Traditional Indian Cookery

By the same author

Indian Vegetarian Cookery

Traditional
Indian
Cookery

JACK SANTA MARIA

Illustrated by Carmen Miranda

SHAMBHALA · BOULDER · 1978

SHAMBHALA PUBLICATIONS, INC.
1123 Spruce Street
Boulder, Colorado 80302

© 1977 Jack Santa Maria
All rights reserved
Illustrations © 1977 Hutchinson Publishing Group
All rights reserved
LCC 78-58227
ISBN 0-87773-143-8 cloth
    0-87773-138-1 paper

Library of Congress Cataloging in Publication Data

Santa Maria, Jack.
    Traditional Indian Cookery.

    Published in 1977 under title: Indian meat
and fish cookery.
    Bibliography: p.
    1.   Cookery, Indic.   I.   Title.
TX724.5.I4S28   1978   641.5'954   78-58227
ISBN   0-394-50356-2   (Random)
ISBN   0-394-73547-1   (Random)   pbk.

Distributed in the United States by Random House

Printed in the United States of America

OM. To the Mother of all cooks

'Come hither to us, O Food, auspicious with auspicious help, health-bringing, not unkind, a dear and guileless friend.'

(From a hymn addressed to Pitu (Nourishment, whether food or drink) – Rigveda I. 187)

Contents

8

Fish

Acknowledgements

The author wishes to thank the British Museum for permission to reproduce the cover illustration.

My thanks are also due to the following:
My numerous teachers,
Lucy Santa Maria and Eunice Santa Maria.
The late Mrs Biriani, with fond memories.
Kevin McDermott, my editor.
The Royal Asiatic Society.

Introduction

Since ancient times, the taking of nourishment has been part of Indian religious life and ritual. With her centuries-old tradition of religious tolerance, India has become a nation of many religions. Each community has its own special dietary laws which affect what the people may eat, when they may eat it, and how they may prepare it. Until recently, these dietary laws were rigidly adhered to, but with increasing industrialization, urbanization and movement of the people has come a change in eating habits for millions. For some this change may be a loss of religious conviction. For others, convenience foods, packaging and advertising have affected the cuisine.

Aware of these changes, writers in India are trying to rescue as many choice recipes as they can before the knowledge disappears forever. That India had for thousands of years been the home of an excellent and diverse culinary tradition is known through the extensive documentation available both within India and in other countries. For example, Megasthanes, the Greek ambassador of Seleukos to the court of Chandragupta Maurya (302–288 B C), made detailed notes of his observations. In them he says that India supplied food in unsparing profusion and the soil of the country produced fruits of all kinds. In addition to various cereals, including millet and rice, legumes of different kinds were grown throughout India. Famine, he observed, had never occurred in India and food scarcity was unknown.

This book of meat and fish recipes endeavours not to duplicate too much those already available in the West, in particular recipes from Pakistan and the northern states. The cooking habits of India vary not only within the religious communities but from area to area. Recipes are included, therefore, from all over the subcontinent to illustrate the variety of techniques and preparations that are possible. Some vegetable dishes are included here as accompaniments to the main courses, but I would refer you to my *Indian Vegetarian Cookery* if a greater variety of these is required.

In the north, where wheat is grown, breads rather than rice form the staple part of the diet. Here, Moslem cooking techniques dominate all meat and fowl dishes. Islam favours the sheep or goat and many delicious ways of preparing mutton and lamb are 'Mughlai'. The famous tanduri method of baking was originally done in a barrel-shaped clay oven or *tandūr* made out of doors. Pulau rice or khichhari may accompany curries, also specially prepared vegetables. Split peas or dals are eaten at nearly every meal in a variety of forms. Curd (yogurt) is a nourishing addition, along with pickles and chutneys. Desserts and sweetmeats made from milk may follow, especially firni and varieties of khir and halva.

Southern India is noted for its rice dishes and hot curries typified by the Madras cuisine. Coconut is plentiful and features prominently in the cooking. Towards the end of the meal the rice may be mixed with yogurt, which has a cooling effect. Pachadi, seasoned yogurt, like the Northern raita, may also be served. South Indian breakfasts include dosas, pancakes made with various flours, accompanied by chutneys or sambhar, a hot lentil soup. South Indian coffee, which is among the world's best in quality, is drunk with milk and sugar and served at any time of the day.

In western India the food takes on a Gujerati or Maharashtri character. A sweet may be served at the beginning of a meal and is eaten with a puri or chapati, followed by the curry, vegetables and lentils.

In Bengal, where rice and dals are popular, many Hindus eat fish. Bengali or East Indian food is plainer, with rice forming the main part of the meal along with luchchis, a fried bread like a puri. Desserts include milk-sweetened yogurt (*mishti dhoi*) and various milk sweets like sandesh.

According to the yogis of old, food, like other matter, may be classified as possessing three distinct qualities or a mixture of these. These are *tamas*, the quality of inertia and dullness; *rajas*, the quality of action and the excitement of the mind and body; and *sattva*, the quality of harmony and the elevation of the spirit. Certain foodstuffs can be easily classified under one of these headings. Chilli, for example, is an obvious rajasic ingredient. Some ancient authorities go further and classify the root vegetables as tamasic in tendency since they grow underground, in the darkness. Those foods which grow and develop in the air, above ground level, are considered more sattvic. Flesh is usually classified as rajasic, though the authorities seem to disagree in their classification of meat, fowl and fish. The digestive system probably has to work a little harder to digest flesh than fruit or vegetables and most people following an intensive course of yoga tend to give up meat-eating. However, many passages in Indian scripture may be found which warn the adept against making the assumption that merely a change of diet will bring about a change of consciousness. Holy men through the centuries have pointed out the futility of blind adherence to law without understanding. Shiva himself admonished men about the slavish performance of ritual in eating. If it were possible to attain liberation by merely eating grass, then a donkey should be instantly set free, he said.

The *Mahābharata*, in a verse of the Shanti Parva, refers to the necessity of ensuring purity in food and drink as one of the ten essential disciplines of life (273. 15). The *Bhagavad Gītā* distinguishes temperament according to the kind of food we prefer. Those foods liked by the satt-vic personality are savoury and oleaginous, substantial and agreeable, and they increase life, energy, strength, health, joy and cheerfulness. Foods liked by the rajasic are excessively bitter, sour, salty, pungent or dry and burning. They will cause pain, grief and disease, says the *Gītā*. Tamasic people prefer food which is stale, tasteless, rotten or left over. These qualities refer to food that has lost its nutritious value due to bad cooking, faulty preparation or putrefaction (XVII. 8-10).

Each meal, therefore, should be planned as a harmonious one. If much spice or acid is used, balance it with something bland. The meal that leaves us heavy and full of sleep has also filled us with the quality of tamas. An overspiced meal that overstimulates the digestive organs or excites the nervous system is rajasic. Meat should be care-fully balanced with the other items in the diet and never allowed to dominate. In this way we feel contented without being bloated. 'Eat till your stomach is three-quarters full and leave one-quarter for the Lord' is the wise saying that encourages us to fully appreciate the food as well as giving the digestion a chance to operate efficiently.

In India those who follow the Hindu code of *ahimsa* (non-injury) believe this to mean that the avoidance of injury to living beings is a virtue worthy to be practised at all times, even when we feel hungry! Both animals and plants are alive and the avoidance of injury to them in the preparation of our food may involve a philosophical or religious problem for some. Food and eating are nevertheless divine gifts so that the whole affair, from preparation to consumption, should be carried out in a reverential and joyful frame of mind. The Western cook, unlike the peaceful Indian villager, does not have the time to gently stir some sweet dish for several hours, or to roast and grind the spices daily so that they are always fresh for the curry. As far as possible these more lengthy processes have been eliminated in the recipes and the short cuts which the average Indian housewife of the city herself uses have been suggested without losing the authentic feel of the dish.

Traditionally, Indian cooking has been handed down through the generations by demonstration and word of mouth and, as in most other countries, the excellent cook is a priceless treasure acknowledged by all levels of society. The master chef of the ancient courts was esteemed like the master musician, astrologer or painter and was indeed an artist in his own right. The great chefs specialized in certain areas of cooking and separately explored the arts of rice, meat, vegetables, sweetmeats, and so on, till the magical potions of today were realized.

Indian Vegetarian Cookery has been well received both in England and America. This book is a complement to it and is designed for those who also like meat or fish in their diet. If you can approach your cooking in the traditional Indian manner, you will develop both your own culinary knowledge and your feeling about the preparation of food itself. As always, enjoy, experiment, be bold and let simple delight and intuition guide you.

India and Meat

'The animal that is killed is the concept of good and bad, merit and demerit, the animal of duality which is cut asunder with the sword of knowledge by the knower of yoga. The consciousness thus freed merges with the supreme. This is the true eating of meat.' (Lord Shiva to the Mother of the universe – Kularnava Tantra, *Ullasa* V)

A large proportion of the population in the Indian subcontinent abstain from meat-eating. For the Hindus, this abstention is a religious observance, most animals being held sacred, especially the cow. The rest are either vegetarians for economic reasons or because, like many yogis and holy men, they believe it to be the best diet for their chosen way of life. For people in the rest of the world, the pressure to eat less meat grows as land disappears and costs rise. However, many millions in India do eat meat for religious reasons and religion often decides which form the diet shall take. The Moslems and Jews are not permitted to eat pork, though they may be encouraged to eat mutton, while the Christians eat all kinds of meat. Since the fish is the symbol of Christ, many Christians acknowledge this by the regular eating of fish on Fridays. Some Hindus will eat fish, as in Bengal, while others eat eggs, especially if unfertilized.

The evolution of the Indian diet has been influenced by changes in the population of the country and by political as well as religious changes. The hymns of the Aryan invaders, the Rigveda, mention various sacrifices, including the horse and bull sacrifice. The earliest of these hymns are many thousands of years old and were first handed down by word of mouth. They tell us that the principal foods of the Vedic Aryans were barley-flour, rice and other cereals, fruits, and the flesh of animals like goats, sheep, cows, oxen, deer, buffaloes and sometimes horses. They also ate honey, ghee, curds and other milk preparations.

At this time *mamsa* (flesh) was certainly a regular food in India. The god Agni was referred to as the 'eater of ox and cow' (Rigveda VIII, 43,

11) and in the *Aitareya Brahmana* the worshipper is advised to kill a bull or old barren cow for his entertainment. The god Indra was also fond of the cooked flesh of bulls (Rigveda X, 27, 2). By the fourth century BC, the eating of cows had culminated in the slaughter of huge numbers. The *Mahābharata* refers to an ancient king, Rantideva, for whose kitchen two thousand cows were slaughtered each day. It seems he also acquired renown by the distribution of cooked meat and rice among hungry people (206, 10, 11).

The conduct of the court influenced the function of the royal cooks. Indian kings were more or less vegetarian though the ideal image of a king was that of a brave hunter and warrior, epitomized in the story of the Ramayana. His diet therefore tended towards that of the meat-eating warrior caste (the *kshatriyas*). King Ashoka (264–227 BC), who became converted to Buddhism, repeatedly forbade the mass slaughter of animals destined for the royal table and by the end of his reign the killing of any living creature was absolutely forbidden.

There were strong religious reasons in Hinduism against the killing and eating of cows. In the story of Lord Krishna, and incarnation of the god Vishnu, the young Krishna not only loved butter and curds but worked as a cowherd. During this time he was known as Gopala which is still a favourite name, after Krishna, for boys in India today. The yogi-god Shiva has always had as his vehicle a pure white bull, Nandi, the symbol of the mind. Thus encouraged by the Brahmin priesthood and the edicts of King Ashoka, revulsion against the killing of cows spread throughout Hindu India. Their special sanctity is emphasized by the name *aghnya* (not to be slain) and it is recorded that hurting or enticing another to hurt a cow became an offence punishable by death.

As the theory of *ahimsa* (non-injury) was crystallizing, meat and fish became forbidden to the ruling orthodox Brahmanic families, except on a few special occasions. However, from contemporary records and the legislation governing slaughterhouses, butchers' shops, hunting and fishing, it is certain that large numbers of Indians continued to consume both meat and fish. The sage Kautilya prepared a manual of administration for the instruction and guidance of the princes and people of the Mauryan Empire (fourth and third century BC) known as the *Artha Shastra*. In the appropriate section we find that there was an appointment called the Superintendent of Slaughter Houses. Horses, bulls, monkeys, deer, fish in lakes and game birds were under state protection and entry into forest preserves was forbidden. The Superintendent was entitled to exact a certain toll of all beasts of prey, fish, birds and deer captured. This toll on behalf of the state could be from one-sixteenth to one-sixth of the catch. Strict rules governed the selling of meat. Butchers were only allowed to sell fresh and boneless meat which had just been killed and they could be fined for selling under weight. Cattle such as the milch-cow, bull or calf could not be slaughtered and the penalty was a heavy fine. It was forbidden to sell the flesh of animals which had been killed outside the slaughter-houses, also headless, legless or boneless flesh, rotten flesh, and the flesh of animals which had suddenly died (Book II. 26). Finally, as we see in modern India, the eating of beef by Hindus became totally abolished, though the goat and sheep continued for some time to be a principal article of food.

The Moslem invasion of the Punjab in the eighth century A D had spread by the eleventh century to the whole of Northern India, bringing with it a complete change in eating habits. The era of the Great Mughals (1556–1784) brought political unity to India under Islam, though millions still practised their Hindu way of life. Islam prescribes a diet which is *halāl* (legally permitted). If you wish to purchase the meat which is specially slaughtered and prepared according to Moslem law you will need to go to a *halāl* butcher, just as the orthodox Jew goes to the *kosher* butcher. The *Quran* tells believers what they may consume in this way: 'O believers, eat of the good things which we have supplied you with and give thanks to God if you are his worshippers. But that which dies by itself, and blood, and swine's flesh, and that over which any other name than that of God's has been invoked, is forbidden you. But he who partakes of them by constraint, without lust or desire, no sin shall be upon him.' (*Quran*. Sura II – The Cow).

This Islamic legacy introduced new forms of cookery, particularly meat cookery, which embodied techniques from other parts of Asia as well as the Middle East. These techniques have co-existed with the Hindu quite separately and they can be found today in the homes of Indian Moslems as well as in the Islamic states of Pakistan and Bangla Desh. Along with these two large religious communities, the Sikhs, Jews, Parsis and Christians have created their own forms of meat cookery which in turn have been influenced by environmental conditions. Apart from a rich variety of vegetarian food, therefore, India also possesses a treasure house of ideas and experiments for the adventurous meat and fish cook.

Utensils and Serving

From the Indian point of view, since eating is a divine necessity, food must possess this divine nature and the cook acts accordingly. First, he prepares himself for the task in hand. He bathes and purifies himself after ensuring that the kitchen and utensils to be used are clean. Then, all the ingredients are carefully washed, when necessary, and prepared. Tasting the food during the cooking process is usually avoided and the cook comes to know by experience the correct proportions that suit the tastes of the family.

A satisfactory and balanced meal might consist of two or three dishes, one of which may be lentils, rice, some pickles or chutney, yogurt, and a sweet dish. This may be filled out on special occasions by the addition of more meat or vegetable dishes, a greater range of chutneys, and a salad. Finally, nuts and dried or fresh fruit may be passed round with some little dishes of digestives such as fennel seed (sānf), cardamom (elaichi) and a sweet pān mixture. Any one of the range of Indian breads (rotis) may accompany or be substituted for the rice and as these are often made unleavened from wholemeal flour (ātā) they will provide a nourishing change from your rice cookery. Pappadams, thin crispy biscuits made from gram flour, may be served with rice or rotis.

Traditionally, food is served on a polished circular metal tray (a large one is termed a thal and the smaller individual one a thali) which contains the different dishes and chutneys in separate metal or earthenware bowls. These individual bowls are known as katoris. Rice or bread is kept in the middle of the tray and the diner helps himself to the food in any order he wishes. Lacking these items, the Western cook could easily substitute a set of ordinary china bowls or dishes and a serving plate for each person. Disposable plates were invented long ago in the form of banana leaves and in South India these large leaves are still used for this purpose.

Use heavy pans wherever possible; a deep frying pan is always useful Since stainless-steel covers all uses, this is to be preferred. Keep a separate non-stick pan for sweet things only. A concave iron dish (*tava*) for making chapatis can be purchased at many Asian stores. Wooden spoons are preferable to metal ones; those used for rice, sweet-making and spicy dishes kept for each of these uses only. Separate chopping boards should be kept for fish, meat, vegetables and spices, and nuts and sweet ingredients. A range of metal sieves and a colander will come in handy at all times. A pestle and mortar is a necessity but care should be taken to ensure that no acids or strong alkalis come in contact with a metal one. The ones I have found the most useful and the cheapest to buy are made in India and cut from stone, left slightly roughened. A good grinder could be used for these purposes and blender/liquidizers are also useful tools. However, if these gadgets are used, you must be prepared to go without the satis- faction of being more involved in the cooking process!

The Spices

For many years the Chinese pilgrim Hsuan-Ch'uang was a guest of the emperor Harsha of Kanauj (630–644), and he was fascinated by everything he saw. From his detailed records we are able to put together a vivid picture of the eating habits of the time. Meat dishes and vegetables cooked in oil, he tells us, were well seasoned with various *māsalas* (spice mixtures). These included chilli, cardamom, cloves, cumin and salt. Spices were handed around to stimulate the palate and to encourage thirst. These were various roots, basil (*parnāsa*), asafoetida (*hingu*), ginger (*ardraka*), and andropogon (*bhustrina*). Garlic and onions were forbidden, however, and their indulgence had to take place outside the town!

CARDAMOM (*elaichi*): This member of the ginger family (*Elettaria cardamomum*) is a pungent aromatic, often chewed after eating as a digestive and breath-sweetner, and a primary ingredient in *garam masāla*. It may be used whole in pods or the seeds removed and crushed or ground. The white pods are generally used in sweet things and the green ones in other preparations like meat and fish.

CHILLI (*mirch*): The seed pods of *Capsicum annum* and the pungent seeds. When fresh they are green or red. The dried red pods are used whole or ground to make chilli powder. Chillies impart a distinct flavour to a dish as well as making it very hot to the tongue. The powder also gives a pleasing red colour to the dish. If chillies are excluded, the red colour may still be retained by adding paprika powder in its place. Paprika is a close relative of the hot chilli, having a distinct flavour like other capsicums, but it does not make the dish hot.

CINNAMON (*dalchini*): The dried inner bark of cassia (*Cinnamomum cassia*) is another ingredient in curries and sweet dishes alike. Being an aromatic, it may be chewed to sweeten the breath and it is said to strengthen the gums. True cinnamon (*Cinnamomum zeylanicum*) has a more delicate flavour than cassia and is not as pungent. This makes it more suitable for sweet dishes.

CLOVES (*laung*): The dried fruit of *Myrtus caryophyllus* has always been the basis of the spice trade. Clove oil is antiseptic and strongly aromatic and an essential ingredient in *garam masāla*.

CORIANDER (*dhania*): *Coriandrum sativum* is an annual plant in the Umbelliferous family like Cow Parsley. Its fresh leaves are used in the same way as parsley is used in the West as a garnish or flavouring agent. Now one of the most commonly used herbs in the world, coriander leaves were used in England up to the time of Elizabeth I. The seeds are highly aromatic and are used ground or whole in curries, pulaus and other savoury dishes.

CUMIN (*jīra*): The seeds of black cumin, *Cuminum nigrum* (*kāla jīra*) and white cumin, *Cuminum cyminum* (*safed jīra*) are used whole or ground in sweet or savoury dishes. The whole seeds are an essential ingredient in certain pulaus. Cumin, like coriander, is a member of the parsley family.

CURRY LEAVES (*kari patta*): The pungent aromatic leaves of *Chalcas koenigii* taste like *garam masāla*. Thrown in whole or broken, they give a characteristic flavour to many South Indian dishes. In Tamil the leaves are referred to as *karuvepila* and in Hindi as *katnim* or *mītha nīm*. They may be dried if purchased fresh and stored in an airtight jar till needed.

FENNEL (*sānf*): The small, elongated green seeds of *Foenculum vulgare* taste like aniseed or liquorice. They are one of the seeds handed round after a meal both as a digestive and as a breath-sweetner, though they are also used in curries.

FENUGREEK (*methi*): The leaves of this plant, *Trigonella fenumgraecum*, have a strong flavour and aroma. Less dried methi should be used than fresh. The lightly roasted seeds are used in curries and influence the texture of a dish.

GINGER (*adrak*): The dried spicy rhizomes of *Zingiber officinalis* are used extensively in all forms of cooking. The fresh root, sometimes called green ginger, is usually preferred to the powder. It is considered an aid to digestion and induces sweating.

GUR is unrefined Indian cane sugar with a crude but individual taste and quality. It is sometimes known as *jaggery*.

MINT (*podina*): The fresh leaves are used in a way similar to that of Western cooking, often as a garnish. It is also an ingredient in fresh chutneys.

MUSTARD SEED (*rai*): A tiny round dark brown seed (*Brassica juncea*) which is highly nutritious. Care has to be taken when frying as the seeds tend to jump from the pan when very hot. The leaf of field mustard, *sarson* (*Brassica campestris*) is cooked like spinach. Mustard oil is used in cooking and pickle making, particularly in Bengal and North India.

POPPY SEED (*khus khus*): 900 000 of these tiny seeds are said to make up a pound ($\frac{1}{2}$ kilo). Their colour ranges from creamy white to grey and black. They stimulate the appetite and tend to thicken sauces. Only seeds of the opium poppy (*Papaver somniferum*) are used.

SAFFRON (*kesha*): This is perhaps the most expensive of all spices. It is the dried stigmata of the saffron crocus, *Crocus sativus*, which have to be harvested by hand. It can colour many thousands of times its own weight of water and is usually soaked in warm water or milk to extract the brilliant yellow colour. Turmeric should not be used as a substitute.

SESAME SEED (*til*): Tiny white, highly nutritious seeds giving a particularly nutty flavour. Sesame oil is a sweet oil used for cooking in some parts of the country.

TAMARIND (*imali*): The seed pod and the attached plant material of *Tamarindus indica* which is soaked in warm water to extract its acidic watery pulp. In most cases it is preferable to vinegar where tartness or piquancy is required.

TANDURI POWDER: A red powder which can be purchased in Asian stores used for colouring and flavouring the meat to be baked in the *tandur* (a barrel-shaped clay oven).

TURMERIC (*haldi*): The dried fleshy root of another member of the ginger family (*Circuma longa*). It contains a bright yellow pigment and the saffron robes of holy men are often dyed with it. To be used for this purpose, it must be made fast or the colour will run. It is a principal ingredient in curries but, like chilli, is one to be respected. The warm and pungent flavour is very strong and too much turmeric will overwhelm and ruin a dish. It is often used to colour rice when thrown into the boiling water after the rice.

Essential Spice Recipes

Book Two of Kautilya's *Artha Shastra* mentions interesting suggestions for the preparation of food along with the ideal diet for men, women and children. He also took the trouble to give exact proportions if the cook was in any doubt: 'For dressing twenty palas of flesh, half a kutumba of oil, one pala of salt, one pala of sugar (*kshara*), two dharanas of pungent substances (*katuka*), spices and half a prastha of curd will be necessary. For any greater quantity of flesh increase the ingredients proportionately. For cooking dried vegetables (*saka*), one and a half times the above substances to be added. For dressing dried fish, twice as much.'

If you are intending to develop your knowledge of Indian cooking, you should avoid the use of 'curry powders' and get used to making your own powders and pastes or masalas as they are known. Like all the other techniques, this is part of the craft. The Tamil word *kari* means a sauce or stew. A curry is prepared by stewing the food with masala, a mixture of spices. This may either be served with the sauce or cooked until dry. The advantage in developing your own range of masalas is that you will quickly obtain the exact taste which your dishes require and leave the stamp of individuality upon them. Masalas are designed to suit the particular ingredients and techniques indicated in the recipes. As the recipes show, various forms of specific spices are mixed in special ways to produce the result. The substitution of a blanket curry powder for these special mixtures will obviously produce a completely different result. Like curry powder, the masalas listed below may be purchased already made up but these cannot match the fragrance and freshness of the home-made product.

It is worth while grinding the spices together from the whole seed when making up a masala. Sometimes this may involve grinding them with garlic, ginger or some other plant. Compare the result with using the pre-powdered ingredients. You may feel that it is more satisfying to take a little time and trouble to get the subtlety and freshness that home-grinding gives to your dish. If a recipe suggests this procedure, you can alternatively use powders and chop the other spices if speed and convenience are required.

GARAM MASALA is a condiment added to a dish at a late stage in the cooking, often just before serving. Sometimes it is used as a flavouring agent in cold dishes such as *raitas*. A simple garam masala may be made by grinding $\frac{1}{2}$ cup of green cardamom seed, 1 cup cumin seed and $\frac{1}{2}$ cup of cloves. Mix together and store in an airtight jar. Two more garam masala recipes are given below:

1. Grind together 3 parts cardamom seed, 3 parts cinnamon, 1 part cloves, 1 part cumin seed.
2. Grind together 4 parts black peppercorns, 4 parts coriander seed, 3 parts cumin seed or fennel seed, 1 part cloves, 1 part cardamom seed, 1 part cinnamon.

Bay leaf, nutmeg and mace feature in the recipes of some cooks. As may be seen from the above ingredients and their proportions, the final taste and aroma of the masala is a matter of personal choice and any number of variations can be made up from some sixteen different spices.

Kashmir has developed its own cooking style which has been influenced by Mughal culture. A simple recipe for Kashmiri garam masala is given here and should be used where the recipe calls for this particular masala:

Grind together 4 parts cardamom seed, 3 parts cumin seed, 1 part black peppercorns, 1 part cinnamon, 1 part cloves. Add a pinch of mace and nutmeg and store. Sometimes chilli and salt are added to this recipe with a few drops of water. The masala then approaches the consistency of a paste and may be taken as it is and used as a condiment like a pickle or a chutney.

In South India a particular masala known as *sambhar* or Madras Rasam is used. Fry the ingredients separately before grinding and mixing: 4 parts split black beans (*dāl urhad*), 4 parts coriander seed, 4 parts cumin seed, 2 parts black peppercorns, 1 part fenugreek seed. A hotter sambhar, imparting a quite different flavour, can be made by grinding and mixing 1 part crushed curry leaves with 1 part mustard seed, 1 part fenugreek seed, 1 part cumin seed, 6 parts coriander seed, 6 parts dry red chillies and 1 part black peppercorns.

Basic Ingredients

GHEE: Ghee is clarified butter or margarine in which the water and any impurities have been driven off by heating. Good-quality ghee is available in tins and vegetable ghee is also of excellent quality. If you want to make your own, place either butter or margarine in a pan and simmer for about an hour very gently. Strain and store in a jar or clean tin. Ghee is the traditional cooking medium of India from Vedic times when it was known in Sanskrit as *ghrit*. Mustard oil and sweet (sesame) oil are the main cooking oils in use in certain regions of the country and each imparts its own particular flavour to the dish. Safflower, peanut or any other oil or animal fat may be substituted where ghee is indicated in the recipes.

KHOYA: If fresh milk is boiled in a heavy pan for an hour or so, stirring to prevent sticking, a thick residue results. This khoya is the basis of many sweetmeats, though the cooking process is laborious. Khoya may be made from full-cream powdered milk by working 1½ tablespoons of hot water into every 2 tablespoons of powder to make 85 g. (3 oz.) of khoya.

DAHI: Curd or yogurt is home-made by the country people. The dahi-seller deals in this commodity alone and makes it in enormous bowls. Plain, commercial yogurt is a handy substitute. To make 500 ml. (2 pints) of yogurt you need 500 ml. (2 pints) of milk and 3 heaped tablespoons of commercial yogurt. Heat the milk till it almost boils. Pour it into a bowl and allow to cool till nearly lukewarm (the milk should still feel hot but not burn the skin). If the milk is too hot the culture grows faster and the curd is thicker and tougher. Gently stir in the yogurt at room temperature, cover the bowl and place on a warm blanket. Wrap the blanket round the bowl and leave to stand for at least five hours then put in the refrigerator. Always keep half a cup of yogurt to use as a culture for the next batch. If your yogurt becomes too thin buy some more fresh supply. A simple incubator can be made by fitting a small box with an electric bulb to give a temperature of 43°C and a place to store a bowl of curd. Once a routine is established, real yogurt can be enjoyed in the home every day.

Curd is used in India as an ingredient in cooking and is also eaten as it is along with the food. It is readily digested and is a nourishing accompaniment to any meal. Its slightly tart flavour makes a pleasing change or substitute for a more acid pickle or chutney.

CHENNA: Indian cottage cheese is made by putting dahi in a muslin bag and allowing it to drip overnight until the excess water is removed. If this cheese is pressed with a heavy weight till it hardens, the result is known as *panir*. Panir is cooked in cubes with vegetables and is, like chenna, an ingredient in certain sweetmeats. It is a favourite in the north where *matar panir* curry (peas and panir curry) is popular.

FLOURS, ATA, BESAN and RICE FLOUR: Ata is a whole-grain wheat flour which can only be bought in Asian grocers or health-food stores since it is not the wholemeal flour sold by English bakers. When mixed with water it often takes on a distinctly sticky consistency.

When gram is ground the flour is known as *besan*. Many other members of the pea and bean family are made into a flour in India for use in pastry, batters, pancakes and as ingredients in certain dishes. These flours will be popular with health-food enthusiasts since they contain the whole grain and have nothing added to them. They are also rich in protein.

Rice flour is used both in sweets where it functions like cornflour in Western dishes of a similar nature, and in pancakes and chapatis. A nourishing pancake (*dosa*) is made for breakfast in South India in which rice flour and various gram flours may be used.

COCONUT PRODUCTS: Coconut is used in Western and Southern style cooking. Make two holes in the natural depressions at the top of the coconut. Pour off the water. Tap round the middle of the shell with a hammer till it breaks in half. The white flesh can now be grated, chopped or squeezed.

Coconut milk is made by extracting the juice from the white flesh. This process may be speeded up by adding a little hot water to the coconut flakes. It is always preferable to use fresh coconut, but creamed coconut is a great time-saver. You can buy this as a block which is cut up and hot water added to make the coconut milk. Where grated coconut is called for in the recipe, again, for convenience, desiccated coconut from a packet may be used.

Weights and Measures

The simple weights and measures in the recipes are provided as a starting point for your own experimentation. These may be varied according to taste. The Indian housewife is used to guessing the amounts of the various ingredients and she only uses more accurate measuring when preparing larger quantities of food. Even then she will tend to judge by hand and sight according to the amount of raw materials available. In one family, two cooks using the same ingredients and same quantities will still produce different results and this is all part of the fascination. Try combinations of dishes that suit your taste but always aim at a light and balanced meal.

Here is a comparison between Metric and Imperial systems:
   approximately ½ litre (500 ml.) = approximately 18 fluid oz.
   approximately 30 grams   = approximately 1 oz.
   approximately 450 grams   = approximately 1 lb.

The cup measurement in this book is one which holds 250 ml. (8 fluid oz.) of water, 250 g. (8 oz.) of sugar, 140 g. (5 oz.) of flour, 170 g. (6 oz.) rice.

A teaspoon holds approximately 5 ml. (⅛ fluid oz.), a dessertspoon approximately 15 ml. (½ fluid oz.) and a tablespoon approximately 30 ml. (1 fluid oz.), 30 g. (1 oz.) of ghee or sugar.

All measures are level ones. Though spoon and cup sizes vary, the intelligent cook will soon find out the amounts needed to obtain the desired results. In most cases the recipes are sufficient for 4–6 people.

Tales of Deviprasad:

The Whiteness of Rice and the Yellowness of Saffron

Sometimes the celebrated cook Deviprasad was approached by boys wishing to learn the secrets of his art. So far had his fame travelled abroad that some of these would-be apprentices came from great distances seeking a position in the kitchen. Much of Deviprasad's teaching was by example and while demonstrating his art he rarely spoke. Yet no matter how many mistakes the boys made it was also well known that he rarely ever lost his temper. Truly it could be said that he showed more love to those who toiled in vain than to his brighter pupils who quickly grasped the various principles of cookery. For some reason, Deviprasad's effortless show of love thoroughly annoyed the most advanced of all the apprentices.

One day the boy took a friend aside and asked him 'If I abused our master Deviprasad, he wouldn't be angry, would he? He would return my anger with love wouldn't he?' 'I have never seen any of us show anger to our master,' his friend replied. 'Well, I've watched him. He certainly won't be angry with me. If that's a way of receiving his love I'll abuse him and see what happens!' His friend's face clouded. 'Are you mad, Gopal? You are Deviprasad's finest pupil. You already know how much he cares about you.' Gopal's eyes glowed. 'I'm sick of it. I'm sick of his never-ending love. I'm sick of the way he treats those idiot boys, they're worse than jackals, they'll never be great cooks!'

Thus Gopal chose his moment. As he and Deviprasad were out walking in the fields one day, he began his abuse, carefully watching his master's face. Deviprasad's eyebrows rose for a moment in surprise, then his eyes became filled with sadness as he listened in silence till Gopal had exhausted his bitterness. At last he spoke. 'I see that after all our years together you wished to give me something today, Gopal. But tell me, my son, if a man declined to accept a present made to him, to whom would the present belong?' 'What? Why, the man who first offered it of course.' 'Then, my son, you have abused me but I decline to accept your abuse. I ask you instead to keep it yourself. As such it will cause you suffering as surely as whiteness belongs to rice and yellowness to saffron.' Gopal was speechless for a moment and struggled to reply. Deviprasad raised his hand and continued. 'Feel this wind that blows from heaven. Do you feel it?' 'Yes, master,' Gopal swallowed. 'Well, then, the unseeing one who abuses his loving friend is like a man who clears his throat and spits against the wind. Heaven is surely not abused, but the spittle returns to defile the spitter.'

Rice

The staple food of millions of Asians has, like wheat, many varieties. Twenty-six kinds of rice are noted in the *Padmavat* of Malik Mohammad Jayasi in 1540. The most popular strains used in savoury cooking are the long-grained ones of the Patna type. Basmatti rice is considered the best and most of the crop is grown in fields fed by the sacred rivers which rise in the Himalayas. Whatever the technique to be used in cooking, always soak and wash the rice beforehand in at least three separate washings.

Plain boiled rice is the main item of food in south India and Bengal and Assam in the north-east as it has been since the time of the Vedic Aryans. Pulau brought by the Mughals, Persians and desert men of the west has since become popular all over the country. The tantalizingly elusive fragrance and flavour of a well-prepared pulau is an international language known throughout northern India and the Middle East.

Grains of rice, symbolizing prosperity, wealth and fertility, are sprinkled during *pujas* (acts of worship). Diagrams drawn during various religious rites are frequently made in coloured rice powders, and decoration in this medium has become an art form in its own right. It is considered auspicious to fill the bowl of a wandering holy man (*sādhu*) with some cooked rice and the Hindu priest is sometimes presented with a bag of rice after conducting a religious ceremony.

Plain Rice (*Chāval*)

There are many ways of preparing plain boiled rice but they all benefit from the rice having been soaked in water before cooking. Soaking time may vary from five minutes to a few hours. Always wash the rice thoroughly before leaving it to soak.

While a guest of the emperor Harsha of Kanauj, the seventh-century Chinese pilgrim Hsuan-Ch'uang made copious notes on rice cooking. To cook rice, he said, a wood fire was lit over a few stones with logs bought from the foresters who sold them at the gates of towns and villages. A cauldron was placed over the flames, then filled with water in the proportions three of water to one of rice. When the water was boiling, the rice, frequently rinsed beforehand, was thrown in and allowed to boil for fifteen minutes. During this time the scum forming on the surface was skimmed off and the rice was stirred so that it should not stick to the bottom of the pot. When it was ready, the rice was carefully drained, heaped on to a tray supported by a rattan stand and cooled with a little flag-shaped fan. The rice was served with curds and three spices, carefully ground – cinnamon, cardamom and mace – or served flavoured with ghee, mango juice or a sauce made with gram (probably some kind of dal preparation). This simple and mouth-watering account could be duplicated by anyone visiting a village today, even down to the rattan stand and flag-shaped fan!

The simplest technique is to empty 1½ cups of washed and drained rice into a pan of boiling water with 1–2 teaspoons of salt. In 10–12 minutes the rice should be ready, the grains tender but firm. Pour into a metal colander and leave to drain. The grains should be separate from each other, not mushy and stuck together. In parts of the North West Frontier Region, the boiled rice is drained and returned to the pan with 2 tablespoons of ghee or butter and a teaspoon of cumin seeds or powder. This makes the rice a little rich and spicy. Stirring in some cooked vegetables or small pieces of meat or fish can, in the same way, make your plain rice more interesting.

Five Spice Rice (*Pānch pūran chāval*)

Plain boiled rice can be made both rich and colourful by adding nuts, sultanas and five spices (*pānch pūran*), and colouring the grains with turmeric powder. Fry half a cup of finely chopped onion, cashew nuts and sultanas separately. In South India, grated coconut would be added along with the nuts and sultanas. Stir into the cooked and drained rice. Fry half a teaspoon each of fennel seeds, cumin seeds, fenugreek seeds, poppy seeds and mustard seeds with a teaspoon of turmeric powder in 2 tablespoons of ghee. Stir into the rice and mix well till all the rice has become yellow. Other seeds such as sesame and caraway go equally well in such a mixture which may be varied according to taste.

Plain Pulau Rice

Indian pulau, apart from being very like its Middle Eastern ancestors, has relations in Spain and Italy also – the paella and risotto.

The simplest savoury rice is made by frying 1½ cups of washed and drained rice in a tablespoon of ghee for a few minutes. First the grains become translucent, then white and opaque. Add 3 cups of boiling water and 1½ teaspoons of salt. Bring to the boil, cover and simmer gently till all the liquid is absorbed. This last part of the process may be finished off in a moderate oven. The grains should be tender and separate. A tastier plain pulau can be made using the following ingredients:

1½ cups rice
2 tablespoons ghee
1 onion, sliced
4 cloves garlic, finely chopped
3 cm. (1 inch) piece ginger,
  finely chopped
6 cloves
5 cm. (2 inches) cinnamon,
  broken

½ teaspoon paprika or chilli
  powder
2 green cardamoms
1 teaspoon garam masala
1 teaspoon cumin seeds
1½ teaspoons salt
3 cups water or stock, hot
chopped fresh coriander leaves
  for garnish

Fry half the onion with the garlic in ghee till golden. Add the rest of the ingredients and the drained rice and stir till the grains become opaque. Add the boiling water or stock, bring to the boil, cover and simmer gently till all the liquid is absorbed and the rice is cooked. Meanwhile fry the rest of the onion to garnish with the chopped coriander leaf.

Peas Pulau (*Matar pulau*)

This can be made in the same way. Add 1½ cups of fresh peas at the beginning of the frying or, if frozen, at the end: this prevents them becoming too soft. Fry a sliced onion and 10 almonds and use to garnish with a sliced hard-boiled egg, sliced tomatoes, cucumber and chopped coriander leaves. Serve with a curry and beaten yogurt.

Nine Gem Rice (*Navratan chāval*)

This pulau, introduced by the Great Mughals, is sometimes coloured with red and green colouring. Navratan refers to the nine gems of the Emperor Akbar.

1½ cups rice
3 tablespoons ghee
1 onion, finely chopped
6 cloves garlic, finely chopped
8 peppercorns
6 cloves, 2 bay leaves
4 green cardamoms
3 cm. (1 inch) piece cinnamon,
  broken

1 cup cauliflower pieces
½ cup peas
½ teaspoon turmeric powder
1½ teaspoons salt
1 tablespoon almonds, blanched
  and sliced
1 tablespoon cashew nuts
1 tablespoon pistachio nuts
2 tablespoons sultanas

Wash the rice and leave to drain. Heat the ghee and fry the onion and garlic till golden. Add the spices and fry for a minute then add the vegetables and continue frying for three to four minutes. Add the drained rice and stir until the grains become opaque. Now add 3 cups hot water, turmeric and salt. Cover and simmer till the rice is cooked. Meanwhile fry the nuts and sultanas in a little ghee till golden. Serve hot with a curry and garnish with the nuts and sultanas and some chopped coriander leaf. A few slices of tomato would, of course, add a pleasing red colour to the dish.

Mixed Vegetable Pulau (*Sabzi pulau*)

1½ cups rice	1 carrot, sliced
3 tablespoons ghee	4 green cardamoms
1 onion, finely chopped	6 black peppercorns
1 teaspoon cumin seeds	2 cloves
1 cup cauliflower pieces	1½ teaspoons salt
½ cup peas	½ green capsicum, sliced

Wash the rice and leave to drain. Heat the ghee and fry the onion till golden then add the cumin seeds and fry till they jump. Add the vegetables and the rest of the spices and cook for a few more minutes. Add the rice, salt and capsicum and stir fry till the rice becomes opaque. Add 3 cups of water, cover and simmer till the rice is tender and the vegetables are cooked.

Brinjal Pulau (*Baingan pulau*)

1½ cups rice	½ teaspoon paprika or chilli
ghee	powder
2 onions, chopped	½ teaspoon cumin seeds
2 aubergines	6 cloves
salt	4 cardamoms

Wash the rice and leave to drain. Heat the ghee and fry one of the onions lightly. Wash the aubergines and cut into cubes and add to the onion. Season with salt and the paprika and cook gently till the aubergines are tender. Heat 2 more tablespoons of ghee and fry the second onion till golden. Then add the rice and spices with salt to taste till the grains become opaque. Add 3 cups of hot water and simmer gently till the rice is tender. Before serving, add the cooked aubergines (brinjals).

Meat Pulau (*Pulau gosht*)

1½ cups rice
ghee
2 onions, finely chopped
¼-½ kilo (½-1 lb.) meat, cubed
3 cm. (1 inch) piece ginger, chopped

2 cloves garlic, finely chopped
3 cm. (1 inch) piece cinnamon
4 cloves
salt

Wash the rice and leave to drain. Heat the ghee and fry the onion till golden. Add the meat pieces and fry till the liquid evaporates, then add the rest of the ingredients and a little water to cook the meat. Warm some more ghee in a pan and fry the rice till it becomes opaque and then add 3 cups of hot water or stock. Allow to cook for a few minutes and add the cooked meat with salt to taste. Either cover and continue to cook gently till the rice is ready or put in the oven on a very low heat to allow the water to dry.

Chicken Pulau (*Pulau murgh*)

small chicken, cut in pieces
ghee
2 onions
4 black peppercorns
salt
½ cup mixed nuts, chopped
½ cup sultanas

1½ cups rice, washed and drained
6 cloves
5 cm. (2 inch) piece cinnamon, broken
6 green cardamoms

Wash the chicken and leave to dry. Heat some ghee and fry one chopped onion with the chicken pieces to seal. Drain off any surplus ghee and boil the chicken in a little water with some chopped onion, peppercorns and salt to taste to make a broth for the rice. Meanwhile fry the nuts and sultanas in ghee and keep on one side. Fry another sliced onion and keep on one side also. Fry the rice in some more ghee till opaque then add the chicken broth which should be equivalent to 3 cups of liquid. Put in the cooked chicken pieces and the spices and simmer gently till the rice is tender. Serve on a flat dish with some vegetable and curd and garnish with the fried nuts and sultanas. Sliced hard-boiled egg would also make a nice garnish.

Pathani Pulau

1 chicken
salt
5 cm. (2 inch) piece ginger
4 cloves garlic
250 gm. (½ lb.) potatoes,
    unpeeled, par-boiled
ghee
2 onions, finely chopped
4 green cardamoms
5 cm. (2 inch) piece cinnamon,
    broken
6 cloves
1 bunch spinach
1 tablespoon mint leaves
1 teaspoon turmeric powder
1 teaspoon cumin powder
2 teaspoons coriander powder
1 teaspoon chilli or paprika
    powder
1 cup yogurt
1½ cups rice, par-boiled
2 hard-boiled eggs, sliced

Wash the chicken and cut in pieces. Boil in a little water with some salt and the ginger and garlic. Meanwhile peel the par-boiled potatoes and fry them in a little ghee. Heat 2 tablespoons of ghee and fry the whole spices with the sliced onion till golden. Now add the washed spinach, mint leaves and masala spices. Fry gently for a few minutes. Stir in the curd and add the chicken pieces, fried potatoes and a pinch of salt. Meanwhile nearly cook the rice in the chicken broth and add to the masala chicken when ready. At the same time spoon in a little melted ghee to allow all the ingredients to mix well and cook together. Cover and place in the oven on a low heat for 15–30 minutes. Serve garnished with the egg slices.

Turkey Pulau

¼ kilo (½ lb.) turkey pieces
salt
2 tablespoons ghee
1 onion, chopped
½ teaspoon cumin seeds
1½ cups rice, washed and drained
½ cup almonds, blanched and
    chopped
½ cup sultanas
chopped fresh coriander leaf

Boil the turkey pieces in a little water with some salt and keep the broth. Heat the ghee and fry the onion till golden. Now add the cumin seeds and rice and fry till the rice is opaque. Put in the turkey pieces and fry for two more minutes. Now add the stock which should be equivalent to 3 cups of liquid and cook gently till the rice is tender. Meanwhile fry the nuts and sultanas in a little ghee and keep on one side. When the rice is ready serve garnished with the coriander leaf, nuts and sultanas.

Fish Pulau (*Machchli ka pulau*)

½ kilo (1 lb.) fish fillets
salt
turmeric powder
1½ cups rice, washed and drained
2 tablespoons grated coconut
2 green chillies

1 tablespoon coriander leaf
½ teaspoon cumin seed
½ teaspoon salt
ghee
½ cup coconut milk/creamed
    coconut water

Wash the fish and dust each fillet with a little salt and turmeric powder. Boil the rice with a teaspoon of salt and half a teaspoon of turmeric powder in the water. Drain and keep aside. Meanwhile grind the green chutney ingredients with the grated coconut and salt. Heat a little ghee and lightly fry the chutney for two to three minutes. Lay in the fish fillets, sprinkle with a little water and allow to simmer gently for four minutes. Turn them over and cook the other side for three or four minutes. Now grease a heavy pan and spread half the rice on the bottom and pour half of the coconut milk over it. Arrange the fish on the rice, cover with the rest of the rice. Finally pour on the rest of the coconut milk and a tablespoon of melted ghee. Cover and cook on low heat for ten to fifteen minutes. This pulau is very nice served with some curd and lemon slices or pickle.

Chicken Rice with Peas (*Matar murgh chāval*)

1 chicken
3 tablespoons ghee
2 onions, sliced
4 green chillies
2 tablespoons chopped
    coriander leaf
4 tomatoes, chopped
1½ cups rice, washed and drained
2 cups peas

juice of 1 lemon
6 black peppercorns
salt
1 teaspoon brown sugar
½ cup almonds, blanched and
    chopped
½ cup sultanas
2 hard-boiled eggs, sliced

Wash the chicken and cut into pieces. Heat the ghee and fry 1 onion with the green chillies, coriander and tomatoes. When the onion is golden add the chicken pieces and fry well. Now add 3–5 cups of hot water and allow to simmer. When the chicken begins to get tender add the rice with the peas, lemon juice, peppercorns, salt to taste and brown sugar. Simmer gently till the rice is cooked. Meanwhile heat a little ghee and fry the rest of the onion, nuts and sultanas. Garnish the chicken rice with this and decorate with the hard-boiled egg slices.

Vegetable Biriani

2 cups rice
2 tablespoons ghee
2 onions, chopped
2 tomatoes, chopped
2 cloves garlic, finely chopped
1 teaspoon garam masala
1 teaspoon turmeric powder

4 green chillies
4 green cardamoms
5 cm. (2 inch) piece cinnamon, broken
4 cloves
2 teaspoons salt
½ cup nuts, chopped

Wash the rice and leave to drain. Heat the ghee and fry the onions till golden. Add the tomatoes and fry for a further two minutes. Stir in the rest of the ingredients except the nuts and fry for a few more minutes. Now add the drained rice and fry till it becomes opaque. Pour in 4 cups of hot water and simmer till the rice is cooked. Meanwhile fry the nuts in a little ghee and use to garnish. This dish is excellent with a curry and curd.

Chicken Biriani

2 cups rice
1 small chicken
1 tablespoon coriander powder
1 teaspoon turmeric powder
1 teaspoon poppy seeds
1 teaspoon salt
2 cups yogurt
ghee
1 onion, chopped
2 cloves garlic, chopped
3 cm. (1 inch) piece ginger, finely chopped

6 cloves
4 green cardamons
5 cm. (2 inch) piece cinnamon, broken
½ teaspoon saffron
2 tablespoons warm milk
½ cup sultanas
½ cup almonds, blanched and chopped
1 tablespoon cashew nuts
1 tablespoon pistachio nuts

Wash the rice and leave to soak. Wash the chicken and cut in pieces. Beat the coriander, turmeric, poppy seeds and salt into the curd and marinate the chicken pieces in this mixture. Heat 3 tablespoons of ghee and fry the onion and garlic with the cloves, ginger and carda-moms till golden. Now add the chicken pieces with the curd and allow to cook in its own gravy till tender. Meanwhile soak the saffron in warm milk to extract the colour. Heat two tablespoons of ghee and fry the same amount of onion, garlic and ginger till golden. Add the same amount of whole spices and fry for a further two minutes. Add the drained rice and fry till it becomes opaque. Add a teaspoon of salt, the saffron milk and 4 cups of water and allow to simmer until the rice is cooked. Meanwhile fry the sultanas and nuts in a little ghee. When the rice is ready, stir in the fried sultanas and nuts. Add the chicken, cover the pan and allow the whole to cook together for five minutes.

Mutton Kichhari

½ kilo (1 lb.) mutton chops	4 cloves
1 cup rice	4 green cardamoms
1 cup lentils or dal	5 cm. (2 inch) piece cinnamon,
½ teaspoon cumin seeds	broken
8 black peppercorns	vinegar
2 red chillies	3 tablespoons ghee
1 teaspoon turmeric powder	1 onion, sliced

Wash the mutton and cut in pieces. Wash and soak the rice and dal. Now grind a masala paste with the spices and a few drops of vinegar. Heat the ghee and fry the masala paste for two minutes. Add the meat and stir fry till well browned. Drain the rice and dal. Fry the onion with a little more ghee, add the rice and cook till it becomes opaque. Now add the dal, meat and 3 cups of hot water. Allow to cook gently till the rice and meat are tender. To add extra flavour to the meat, allow it to marinate in the paste for two hours before frying.

Curd Rice (*Dahi bhāt*)

Here is a simple way to cook rice to eat cold in the warm months: 1 cup of rice should be boiled and allowed to cool. Pour on 3½ cups of milk and stir into the rice with a tablespoon of curd. This mixture can now be packed ready for eating. Serve sprinkled with salt.

An interesting dish for serving with a curry and pickles is given below:

2 cups rice	3 green chillies, sliced
2 cups yogurt	3 cm. (1 inch) piece ginger,
ghee	finely chopped
2 teaspoons mustard seed	1 teaspoon salt
1 tablespoon urhad dal	2 cups milk
1 mango	

Wash the rice and boil till cooked, remove and drain. Beat the yogurt. Heat a little ghee and fry the mustard seed and dal till the mustard seeds jump. Beat into the curd. Slice the mango and add to the curd with the chillies and ginger. Sprinkle with salt and pour over the milk. Mix well and serve with a curry or pickles. Dahi bhat comes from South India.

Lemon Rice (*Nimbu bhāt*)

1 cup rice	2 green chillies
½ teaspoon turmeric powder	½ cup grated coconut
½ teaspoon salt	2 tablespoons lemon juice
2 tablespoons ghee	1 tablespoon chopped fresh
2 tablespoons cashew nuts	coriander leaf
½ teaspoon mustard seeds	½ cup coconut milk/creamed
a few curry leaves	coconut water

Wash the rice and allow to cook in water with turmeric and salt till nearly done. Heat the ghee and fry the nuts, mustard seeds, curry leaves and chillies for two minutes. Add the drained rice and stir, frying for a few more minutes. Now add the grated coconut, lemon juice, coriander and coconut milk. Allow to cook gently till all the liquid is absorbed.

Breads

Many of these recipes involve the preparation of a dough. A few precautions will ensure that your results are successful. Atmospheric conditions change and you may find that more flour is needed on damper days. If your dough sticks to the bowl or your hands after adding all the ingredients, keep kneading and adding a little flour at a time until the ball of dough comes away clean. Always knead well till your dough is soft and pliable. Some doughs acquire a silky texture when ready. If the dough contains yeast, be careful not to leave it too long over the stated period since the effect of the yeast will be lost in cooking. When leaving a dough to stand, cover with a damp cloth.

Unleavened Wholewheat Bread
(*Chapātis and Phulkas*)

Phulkas are small chapatis. Elephants are commonly fed chapatis the size of car tyres. Most of the princely states used to keep elephants for ceremonial purposes as well as for work and a certain elephant was in the habit of weighing his chapatis with his trunk. If one turned out to be underweight, the offending chapati was contemptuously flung away. In the same state was an elephant who was very fond of his driver (*mahut*). He demonstrated this affection by always leaving aside a portion of his vegetable and chapati for the beloved mahut.

For 10–15 chapatis, make a flour and water dough with 2 cups of whole-wheat flour (*ātā*). Sift the flour with a teaspoon of salt and add water gradually, mixing until a soft dough is formed. Knead well with the fist, folding and kneading the dough till it is really pliable. Sprinkle with drops of water, cover with a damp cloth and leave to stand for a minimum of thirty minutes. Set the tava (iron hot-plate) on a medium heat to warm up, slightly greased. Before cooking, knead the dough again, break off pellets and roll into walnut-sized balls. Flatten between the fingers, dip in a little flour and roll out thinly and evenly on a floured board. Experts flatten them with a few vigorous slaps between the palms. Put the chapati on the tava. When it is well heated through, the edges begin to turn up. This is the time to turn it over and bake the other side. When the chapati begins to appear bubbly (the water inside is trying to escape as steam and bubbles up through the dough) remove it from the tava and hold over a gas flame, a hot electric ring or under the grill. The chapati should now puff up completely like a ball. As it collapses, transfer to a plate covered with a clean cloth. The whole process should not take more than half a minute. Try to establish a rhythm of work so that you are rolling out the next chapati while another one is baking.

Chapatis are eaten with curries. You can tear off pieces and use them like a spoon. They are ideal for mopping up gravy or sauce. Warm chapatis and butter are excellent for breakfast or tea and I have yet to meet a child who does not relish them with jam or honey.

Buttered Wholewheat Unleavened Bread (*Parāthas*)

2 cups wholewheat flour (ata)   ½ teaspoon salt
about 1 cup water   ghee

Prepare the dough as for chapatis and leave to stand. Put the tava on to warm. Heat the ghee and have some liquid ghee available. Roll out balls of dough using a little dry flour, not too thinly. Spread a spoonful of ghee over, fold over, roll and spread on more ghee. Do this two or three times and finally roll out fairly thin. Grease the tava and bake one side of the paratha. Grease the top and turn to cook the other side. Turn again if necessary to complete the cooking. Parathas take longer to cook than chapatis and care must be taken not to burn them.

A particular paratha is made in Bengal from a plain flour (*maida*) dough. When the ghee is spread on the uncooked circular paratha, a cut is made with a knife from the centre outwards. Using this cut, the paratha is rolled into a cone which is then squashed flat. The plain flour paratha has a heavier texture.

Stuffed Parathas

Make up the dough as for parathas.

For the stuffing:

2 potatoes	1 teaspoon salt
1 tablespoon ghee	½ teaspoon garam masala
1 onion, finely chopped	¼ teaspoon chilli powder
2 tablespoons coriander leaf or fresh herbs, finely chopped	1 dessertspoon lemon juice
15 mm. (½ inch) piece ginger, finely chopped	

Boil the potatoes and when cool, peel and mash. Heat the ghee and fry the onion, herbs and ginger for a few minutes. Add salt, garam masala and chilli powder. Mix in the mashed potato and sprinkle with lemon juice. Fry for two minutes and allow to cool. Roll out the paratha not too thin, spread on ghee and place a tablespoon of stuffing in the centre. Fold up and gently roll out as thin as possible, using a little dry flour. Cook in the usual way. Serve with a curry or curd.

Other combinations of vegetables can be used as a stuffing. Substitute 250 g. (½ lb.) peas and a chopped tomato for the potatoes, for example.

Puffed Fried Bread (*Pūris*)

2 cups wholewheat flour (ata)	½ teaspoon salt
2 tablespoons ghee	ghee for deep frying

Rub the ghee into the flour and salt. Gradually mix in enough water to make a stiff dough. Knead well and make up into small ping-pong-size balls. Heat some more ghee in a small saucepan to nearly smoking point. Turn the heat down to medium. Lightly grease the rolling board and roller. Flatten a dough ball, dip quickly in the hot ghee and roll out thinly on the board. Make sure that the puri is not bigger than the pan. Drop it in the hot ghee and press gently with the back of a spoon. The puri should immediately puff up like a ball. Allow to turn golden, turn and quickly fry the other side.

As in making chapatis, the cooking should be done quickly. A rhythm of work can be established so that you are dipping and rolling out the next puri while the other one is browning in the hot ghee. Puris are eaten with most dishes, especially semolina (sūji), kabli channas and dry curries.

Luchchis are fried breads like puris but plain flour (maida) is used to make the dough. They are a favourite in Bengal. Proceed as for puris frying one at a time in hot ghee.

Flat Baked Bread (Nān)

Emperor Akbar's prime minister, Abul Fazl, compiled an account of the administrative and revenue systems of the time, called the Aiin-i-Akbari. In it is recorded the largest kind of bread to be baked in the royal kitchen. This mighty nan was made of 10 seers (9 kilos/20 lb.) of maida (plain fine wheat flour), 5 seers of cow's milk, 1½ seers of ghee and ¼ seer of salt. The smallest nan can be made using these proportions.

2 cups wholewheat or plain flour	1 tablespoon ghee
½ teaspoon salt	140 ml. (5 oz.) milk

Sift the flour with the salt and rub in the ghee. Gradually mix in the milk and enough water to make a soft dough. Form into flat cakes about 30 cm. (12 inches) across and 6 mm. (¼ inch) thick. Bake in a hot oven till light brown and crisp.

Nans are ideal for stuffing. Make a slit in the side and fill with a seasoned salad, vegetables or meat in a savoury sauce.

Semolina Puris (*Sūji pūri*)

3 cups wholemeal flour
4 tablespoons gram flour
  (besan)
2 tablespoons semolina (suji)

1 teaspoon salt
¼ teaspoon chilli powder
2 tablespoons ghee

Mix the flour and semolina. Add the salt and chilli powder and the ghee. Gradually add enough water to make a stiff dough. Cover with a damp cloth and leave for an hour. Knead again and cook as for puris.

Stuffed Puris (*Pithi pūri*)

Make up a dough as for puris with 2 cups of flour.

For pithi:

½ cup urhad dal
3 cm. (1 inch) piece ginger,
  finely chopped
2 cloves garlic, chopped

¼ teaspoon chilli powder
salt to taste
lemon juice
ghee for deep frying

The dal needs to soak for four hours. Drain and grind together with the rest of the ingredients, adding a few drops of lemon juice to make a dry paste. Roll out the dough in the normal way. Put in a teaspoon of the pithi and roll up. Using a little dry flour roll out again carefully without breaking the puri. Deep fry in the usual way. Serve hot or cold.

Tanduri Bread (*Tandūri roti*)

Make up a dough as for chapatis. Roll out each ball and spread with a little ghee. Roll up, do this again and shape into small flat breads. Smear the top with melted ghee and sprinkle with sesame seed and a little garam masala. Cook on the tava till half done then put under the grill to toast to a nice brown colour.

Spicy Pancake (*Masāla dosa*)

½ kilo (1 lb.) rice flour
3 tablespoons urhad dal flour
1 teaspoon salt
ghee
1 onion, finely chopped
4 cloves garlic
3 cm. (1 inch) piece cinnamon
2 cloves
½ teaspoon cumin seeds

½ teaspoon mustard seeds
1 teaspoon urhad dal
3 cm. (1 inch) piece ginger,
    finely chopped
2 green chillies, sliced
a few curry leaves
½ teaspoon turmeric powder
2 potatoes, cooked and mashed

Mix the flours and salt, adding enough warm water to make a thick batter. Leave to stand for an hour. Heat a tablespoon of ghee and fry the onion till golden. Meanwhile grind the garlic, cinnamon, cloves and cumin seeds adding a few drops of water to make a paste. Fry the mustard seeds and urhad dal till the mustard jumps. Now stir in the garlic paste, ginger, chillies, curry leaves and turmeric and fry for two minutes. Add the potato and fry for a few more minutes. The filling is now ready for the dosas, keep on one side. Heat a tava or heavy pan and wipe with a little ghee. Drop on some of the batter to make a thin pancake. When the underside begins to turn golden spoon a little melted ghee around the edges and turn the dosa over. Cook till the other side turns golden and remove. Place some of the filling on one end of the dosa and roll up. Keep on a plate and serve with coconut chutney. Keep the tava clean between cooking each dosa.

Spiced Bread (*Thalipīt*)

2 green chillies
4 cloves garlic
2 tablespoons coriander leaf
2 teaspoons cumin seeds
2 tablespoons coriander seeds

2 cups rice flour
1 cup urhad dal flour
½ cup gram flour (besan)
salt
4 tablespoons ghee

Grind the chillies, garlic, coriander leaf, cumin and coriander seeds. Mix with the flour with salt to taste. Rub in the ghee and add enough water to make a stiff dough. Divide the dough into balls and shape each ball into a thick, round roti. Heat a tava, grease and cook the rotis on a gentle heat. Remove when cooked and smear with butter. This bread from Maharashtra is delicious with raita.

Cornflour Pancake (*Makai dosa*)

1 tomato, finely chopped
1 onion, finely chopped
1 tablespoon coriander leaves
   chopped
2 green chillies, finely sliced

½ cup cornflour
½ cup gram flour
½ teaspoon salt
ghee

Mix all the ingredients together except the ghee and add enough water to make a thick batter. Heat a tava and spread with ghee. Pour on about two tablespoons of the batter and cook till the underside turns golden. Put a little melted ghee round the edge and turn to cook the other side. Serve with a fresh chutney.

Meat

The Chinese pilgrim, Hsuan-Ch'uang (seventh century), tells us
that in India useful animals were never killed, nor those giving milk,
except gazelles. When meats were boiled, he noted, they were flavoured
with the juice of fruits or bitter herbs (*amlavarga*) such as lemon,
orange, pomegranate (*dādima*), tamarind and sorrel (*chukra*). Or the
meat was cut in slices and fried in ghee, sesame oil or mustard oil.
Sometimes whole briskets, smeared with ghee and sprinkled with
salt and pepper (*maricha*), were cooked in this way. Birds were wrapped
in bitter leaves and roasted, served with a thick sauce made of ghee,
mango juice, salt and pepper. Succulent carps were also served at such
meals. The *Harivamsha* (a supplement to the *Mahābharata*) tells of
banquets where the guests were offered whole animals roasted on the
spit whose juicy meat was basted with melted ghee and served floating
in a spicy sauce made of sour fruits and salt.

Beef

Beef Curry

2 tablespoons coriander seeds
1 teaspoon turmeric powder
½ teaspoon cumin seeds
6 peppercorns
2 red chillies
3 cm. (1 inch) piece ginger
4 cloves garlic
3 tablespoons ghee

1 onion, sliced
½ kilo (1 lb.) beef, washed and
    cut in cubes
3 tablespoons grated or
    desiccated coconut
½ cup tamarind water
salt

Grind the spices, ginger and garlic to form a paste, adding a little water if necessary. Heat the ghee and fry the onion till golden. Add the masala paste and fry for a further two minutes. Now add the meat and fry till well browned. Stir in the coconut and pour over the tamarind water. Sprinkle with salt to taste and simmer gently till the meat is tender, adding a little more water if necessary to form a gravy.

Madras Bafat

¾ kilo (1½ lb.) beefsteak, sliced
5 potatoes, quartered
3 carrots, sliced
3 radishes, sliced
8 spring onions, sliced
2 dry red chillies
½ teaspoon mustard seed
½ teaspoon cumin seed

2 teaspoons turmeric powder
1 dessertspoon coriander seed
4 green chillies
3 cm. (1 inch) piece ginger
2 cloves garlic
salt
vinegar

Put the steak and vegetables in a pan and cover with water and boil gently. Grind the masala ingredients in the meantime and stir into the meat with salt to taste. Add two tablespoons or more of vinegar when the meat and vegetables are cooked. Serve with rice.

Beef Masala Fry

1 tablespoon coriander seed
3 cm. (1 inch) piece cinnamon
4 cloves
2 green cardamoms
½ teaspoon cumin seeds
2 dry red chillies
½ teaspoon poppy seed
½ teaspoon turmeric powder
3 cm. (1 inch) piece ginger
4 cloves garlic
2 tablespoons ghee

1 onion, sliced
250 g. (½ lb.) beef, washed and
  cubed
salt
4 tablespoons grated or
  desiccated coconut
250 g. (½ lb.) mixed vegetables
  chopped
juice of ½ lemon or tamarind
  water

Grind the spices, ginger and garlic. Heat the ghee and fry the onion till golden. Add the masala paste and fry for a further two minutes. Put in the meat and brown nicely. Sprinkle with salt to taste and add the coconut and vegetables. Fry for a few minutes and then add the acid and a little water if necessary. Simmer gently till the meat is tender.

Frithath Curry

½ teaspoon cumin seed
10 peppercorns
2 dry red chillies
1 teaspoon turmeric powder
4 cloves
4 green cardamoms
5 cm. (2 inch) piece cinnamon
1–2 tablespoons vinegar
3 tablespoons ghee

1 onion, sliced
2 green chillies, sliced
6 cloves garlic, sliced
3 cm. (1 inch) piece ginger,
  sliced
½ kilo (1 lb.) beef, washed and
  cubed
salt
tamarind water

Grind the spices and add the vinegar slowly to make a paste. Heat the ghee and fry the onion till golden. Add the green chillies, garlic and ginger and fry for two minutes. Put in the meat and brown nicely. When the gravy begins to evaporate, keep the heat low and add the masala paste and fry for three minutes. Sprinkle with salt to taste and a little tamarind water. Simmer gently till the meat is tender.

Beef Stew

1 kilo (2 lb.) beef
salt and pepper
3 tablespoons ghee
4 radishes, sliced
3 carrots, sliced
4 spring onions, sliced

5–6 potatoes, chopped
3 cm. (1 inch) piece ginger,
    finely chopped
2 green chillies, sliced
a few mint leaves

Cut the meat in pieces, sprinkle with salt and pepper and brown in ghee. Remove from the pan, add some more ghee and fry the vegetables with the ginger, green chillies and mint leaves. Put in the meat, cover with water and stew gently till the meat is tender and the vegetables are cooked. The gravy may be thickened by adding a dessertspoon of cornflour in a little warm water. Stir occasionally.

This dish can be varied by cooking the meat with ½ kilo (1 lb.) of Lady Fingers cooked whole; when the vegetable is cooked add the juice of half a lemon.

Brown Stew

1 onion, sliced
3 tablespoons ghee
½ kilo (1 lb.) beef, washed and
    cubed
3 cm. (1 inch) piece ginger,
    finely chopped
3 cm. (1 inch) piece cinnamon,
    broken

6 cloves
2 tomatoes, sliced
1 teaspoon paprika or chilli
    powder
½ kilo (1 lb.) mixed vegetables,
    chopped
2 tablespoons vinegar
salt

Fry the onion in ghee till golden. Add the meat and brown nicely. Now add two cups of hot water and the spices and tomato. Stir and cook for a few minutes, then add the vegetables and vinegar. Sprinkle a little salt to taste and allow the dish to simmer until all the meat and vegetables are cooked. The gravy may be thickened with cornflour in warm water if desired. Serve with chapatis or other breads.

Curd Beef (*Korma gosht*)

1 teaspoon turmeric powder
2 tablespoons coriander leaves
1 green chilli
3 cloves garlic
3 cm. (1 inch) piece ginger
5 cm. (2 inch) piece cinnamon

1 cup yogurt
3 onions, sliced
½ kilo (1 lb.) beef, washed and
   cubed
3 tablespoons ghee
salt

Grind the spices to form a paste. Mix well with the curd and put in a dish with two of the sliced onions. Put in the meat mix thoroughly and allow to stand for two hours. Heat the ghee and fry the other onion till golden. Add the meat and curd mixture, season with salt to taste and cook gently till the meat is tender. This dish is nice with either rice or breads.

Spiced Beef (*Masāla gosht*)

½ kilo (1 lb.) beefsteak
3–4 tablespoons vinegar
1 clove garlic, sliced
3 cm. (1 inch) piece ginger,
   finely chopped

3 tablespoons ghee
1 onion, sliced

Wash the steak and beat flat. Cut in pieces and steep in the vinegar, garlic and ginger for six hours. Heat ghee and fry gently till cooked. Add some onion and fry till golden. A little water may now be added if any more gravy is required.

Cumin Beef (*Jīra mīra*)

3 tablespoons ghee
1 onion, sliced
½ kilo (1 lb.) beef, cut in pieces
3 cm. (1 inch) piece ginger,
   finely chopped
2 cloves garlic, finely chopped

½ tablespoon cumin powder
½ teaspoon black pepper
½ teaspoon turmeric powder
salt
2 tablespoons vinegar

Heat the ghee and fry the onion till golden. Add the meat and spices and brown the meat gently. Sprinkle in salt to taste. Add the vinegar and a little water and cook gently till the meat is ready. Serve with vegetable and curd.

Calcutta Beef Curry

2 onions, sliced
2 tablespoons coriander seed
1 teaspoon turmeric powder
½ teaspoon cumin seed
6 peppercorns
2 red chillies

3 cm. (1 inch) piece ginger
4 cloves garlic
3 tablespoons ghee
½ kilo (1 lb.) beef, washed and
     cut in cubes
salt

Grind the onions with the spices, ginger and garlic to form a paste. Heat the ghee and fry the paste for two minutes. Add the meat and brown nicely. Add a little water to enable the meat to be cooked on a low heat. Add salt to taste. Serve with rice and slices of fresh lemon.

Beefsteak Curry

½ kilo (1 lb.) beefsteak
salt
pepper
1 teaspoon turmeric powder
½ teaspoon cumin powder
ghee

½ cup tamarind water
vinegar
4 green chillies, sliced
1 clove garlic, sliced
3 cm. (1 inch) piece ginger,
     finely chopped

Slice the beef and beat to make tender. Sprinkle with salt and pepper, turmeric and cumin. Heat a little ghee and fry the meat till nicely browned. Mix the tamarind water with 1–2 tablespoons vinegar and stir in with the chillies, garlic and ginger. Cover the pan and simmer gently till the meat is tender. Serve with rice and vegetables.

Beef Vindalu

½ kilo (1 lb.) beef, cubed
vinegar
½ teaspoon cumin seeds
8 peppercorns
4 red chillies
2 teaspoons turmeric powder
4 cloves
4 green cardamoms

5 cm. (2 inch) piece cinnamon,
     broken
salt
3 cm. (1 inch) piece ginger,
     finely chopped
4 cloves garlic, finely chopped
ghee

Wash the beef with weak vinegar. Grind the masala ingredients together with some drops of vinegar to make a paste. Rub the paste well into the beef pieces with two-thirds of the masala and place in a bowl. Sprinkle with salt, ginger and garlic. Pour over vinegar enough to just cover and allow to stand for six hours. Warm a little ghee and fry the rest of the masala. Take the beef pieces out of the vindalu marination and add to the fried masala. Cook on a low heat till the meat is tender. Vindalu can be kept in a jar or bowl as long as vinegar or oil covers the meat. No water must be used in the preparation of a vindalu.

Sauteed Beef (*Bhūna gosht*)

¼ kilo (½ lb.) beef
1 teaspoon salt
½ teaspoon chilli powder
4 tomatoes
2 green chillies
2 tablespoons ghee
1 onion, sliced
3 cm. (1 inch) piece ginger, finely chopped

2 cloves garlic, finely chopped
2 green cardamoms
2 cloves
1 teaspoon coriander powder
½ teaspoon turmeric powder
1 teaspoon salt

Wash the meat and cut in pieces. Rub in salt and chilli powder. Grind the tomatoes with the green chillies. Heat the ghee and fry the meat till nicely browned and remove. Now add the onion, ginger and garlic to the ghee and fry for three minutes. Add the spices, cooked meat and the tomato and chilli paste. Stir for a few minutes, then add a cup of water and salt. Cover and cook till the meat is tender, adding more water if necessary. The final dish should be a dry one. Serve with yogurt and puris.

Minced Meat (*Kīma*)

2 tablespoons ghee
2 onions, finely chopped
small piece ginger, finely chopped
¼ kilo (½ lb.) minced beef

½ teaspoon turmeric powder
¼ teaspoon chilli powder
salt
vinegar

Warm the ghee and fry the onion till golden. Add the ginger and the mince and fry for four minutes. Sprinkle on the rest of the ingredients and a cup of water. Allow to cook till the mince is ready on a low heat. This dish may be served dry or add more water to make a gravy.

Minced Meat and Marrow Curry (Kīma gūda)

1 marrow
ghee
2 onions, sliced
1 teaspoon chilli powder
½ teaspoon cumin powder

1½ teaspoons turmeric powder
4 cloves garlic, finely chopped
¼ kilo (½ lb.) minced meat
¼ cup grated or desiccated coconut

Cut the marrow into thick rings and boil in a little salted water till soft. Remove the inside and keep to one side. Heat a little ghee and fry one of the onions till golden. Mix the masala ingredients together and add half to the fried onion. Add the minced meat and fry till browned. Fill the hollowed marrow rings with the mixture and keep warm. Heat more ghee and fry the remaining onion and masala for a few minutes. Add the flesh of the marrow – previously set aside – and the coconut and cook till a thick gravy is formed. Spread over the stuffed marrow rings and serve.

Minced Meat with Green Masala (Kīma masāla)

4 tablespoons coriander leaf
2 green chillies
4 cloves garlic
¼ teaspoon cumin seeds
1 teaspoon turmeric powder

3 cm. (1 inch piece) ginger
1 teaspoon salt
ghee
1 onion, finely chopped
½ kilo (1 lb.) minced beef

Grind the coriander leaves and spices. Add the salt and mix the green paste well with the mince. Heat the ghee and fry the onion till golden. Stir in the mince mixture and fry well till the meat is nicely browned. Add a little water and allow the curry to simmer gently till the meat is cooked.

Minced Meat Kabab (*Shīkh kabāb*)

¼ kilo (1 lb.) minced beef
4 green chillies, finely chopped
2 tablespoons chopped fresh
  coriander leaf
a few mint leaves, chopped
1 onion, finely chopped
4 cloves garlic, finely chopped
3 cm. (1 inch) piece ginger,
  finely chopped

1 teaspoon coriander powder
1 teaspoon cumin powder
1 teaspoon garam masala
1 teaspoon ground cardamom
  seeds
½ teaspoon chilli powder
1 teaspoon salt
juice of ½ lemon

Mix all the ingredients and leave to stand for 3–4 hours. Make the mixture into small balls. Now grease some skewers and shape each ball into a sausage on the skewer or arrange on the grill. Cook gently, basting with ghee till the kababs are well browned and the meat is cooked. Serve with mint chutney and slices of lemon and raw onion.

Mince Uppama

2 carrots, sliced
2 potatoes, quartered
½ cup peas
4 tablespoons ghee
2 cups semolina
2 cloves
3 cm. (1 inch) piece cinnamon
1 teaspoon urhad dal
1 teaspoon mustard seeds
4 green chillies, sliced
3 cm. (1 inch) piece ginger,
  finely chopped

a few curry leaves
1 onion, sliced
¼ kilo (½ lb.) minced meat
1 teaspoon turmeric powder
1 teaspoon garam masala
1 teaspoon salt
2 tomatoes, sliced
juice of ½ lemon
2 tablespoons grated or
  desiccated coconut
chopped fresh coriander leaf

Boil the vegetables in minimum water till tender. Heat the ghee and fry the semolina for four minutes. Add the cloves, cinnamon, dal and mustard seeds. When the mixture begins to turn light red, add the chillies, curry leaves, ginger and onion and fry till the onion is golden. Add the minced meat and vegetables and fry till the meat is nicely browned. Add a cup of water with the turmeric, garam masala, salt and tomatoes. Cook gently till the meat and vegetables are tender. Mix in the lemon juice and coconut and serve garnished with coriander leaf. Serve this Kerala dish with rice and chutney.

Minced Meat with Methi (*Kima methi bāji*)

¼ kilo (1 lb.) methi baji or
  green-leaved vegetable
2 tablespoons ghee
1 onion, finely chopped
¼ kilo (½ lb.) minced meat

2 green chillies, sliced
2 cloves garlic, finely chopped
3 cm. (1 inch) piece ginger,
  finely chopped
salt

Soak the green leaves in water. Heat the ghee and fry the onion till golden. Add the mince, green chilli, garlic and ginger and fry till the mince is browned. Drain the vegetable, chop coarsely and add to the mince. Sprinkle with salt to taste. Cover and simmer for a few minutes till the vegetable is tender.

Small prawns may be used in this recipe instead of the meat.

Mutton and Lamb

Mutton Curry (*Mhāns kari*)

¼ teaspoon cumin seeds
½ teaspoon poppy seeds
2 red chillies
6 cloves garlic
1 teaspoon turmeric powder
½ teaspoon mustard seed
2 tablespoons ghee
1 onion, sliced

½ kilo (1 lb.) mutton, cut in
   pieces
2 green chillies, chopped
3 cm. (1 inch) piece ginger,
   finely chopped
1 tablespoon chopped coriander
   leaf
salt

Grind the masala spices. Heat the ghee and fry the onion till golden. Add the masala and fry for two more minutes. Stir in the meat pieces and brown nicely. Add half a cup of warm water and simmer gently. Stir in the salt, chilli, ginger and coriander leaf. Continue simmering till the meat is tender. This mutton dish is from Madras.

Mahratta Meat Curry

ghee
½ cup grated or desiccated
   coconut
1 teaspoon caraway seeds
1 teaspoon fennel seed
6 peppercorns
5 cm. (2 inch) piece of
   cinnamon, broken
2 green cardamoms
3 cloves
2 red chillies

1 tablespoon coriander seed
1 teaspoon turmeric powder
1 onion, chopped
2 tablespoons coriander leaf
3 cm. (1 inch) piece ginger
2 green chillies
½ kilo (1 lb.) mutton, cut in
   pieces
1 clove garlic, sliced
salt

Heat a little ghee and gently fry the coconut with the dry spices for two minutes. Now grind this mixture with the onion, coriander leaf, ginger and green chillies. Stir in the mutton pieces and brown. Add the garlic and fry for two minutes. Pour in a cup of warm water and salt to taste and simmer gently till the meat is tender.

Curd Lamb (*Mhāns korma*)

¼ teaspoon saffron
2 onions, finely chopped
3 cm. (1 inch) piece ginger, finely chopped
4 cloves garlic, finely chopped
½ teaspoon fennel seed
1 cup yogurt

½ kilo (1 lb.) mutton, cut in pieces
2 tablespoons ghee
salt
¼ cup almonds, blanched and crushed

Put the saffron in a cup with a little warm milk to extract the colour. Stir the onion, saffron and spices into the yogurt and beat well. Put in the mutton pieces to marinate for two hours. Heat the ghee and fry the meat till well browned. Add any remaining yogurt paste and sprinkle with salt to taste with enough water to cook the meat till tender. Just before serving sprinkle with the crushed almonds.

Mutton Bafat

small mutton leg
salt
4 potatoes, chopped
4 carrots, chopped
2 onions, sliced
6 radishes, chopped
1 teaspoon rice flour
1 teaspoon turmeric powder

4 cloves garlic
3 cm. (1 inch) piece ginger
3 red chillies
2 cloves
3 cm. (1 inch) piece cinnamon
ghee
1 onion, finely chopped
vinegar

Simmer the mutton in 3 cups of salted water with the vegetables and keep the broth. Meanwhile grind the masala mixture. Remove the vegetables before they become too soft. Warm a little ghee and fry the other onion till golden. Add the ground masala and fry for two more minutes. Add the meat and brown well. Pour in the broth and sufficient vinegar to taste. When the meat has simmered for a few minutes in the broth add the vegetables and allow to warm through.

Mutton with Egg Sauce (*Andā mhāns*)

2 tablespoons ghee
2 onions, finely chopped
4 cloves
3 cm. (1 inch) piece cinnamon, broken
4 cloves garlic, finely chopped
a few curry leaves
2 red chillies
1 teaspoon fennel seed

½ kilo (1 lb.) mutton, cut in pieces
1 teaspoon turmeric powder
1 egg
½ cup coconut milk (or equivalent creamed coconut)
juice of ½ lemon
2–4 potatoes, chopped and par-boiled

Heat the ghee and fry the onions till golden. Add the spices and fry for a further two minutes. Now put in the washed mutton pieces and brown. Meanwhile, put the turmeric powder in a cup of warm water and mix well. Pour on to the mutton and allow to simmer gently until the mutton is tender. Add a little more water if necessary. While the mutton is cooking, beat the egg, gradually pouring in the coconut milk. Stir in the lemon juice and mix well. Pour the sauce on to the meat and cook for a few minutes. Add the potatoes, cover the dish and simmer till the meat and vegetables are tender. Keep the gravy thick. Serve with chapatis or breads or a biriani rice.

Mutton Stew with Beans (*Mhāns phāli*)

½ kilo (1 lb.) mutton
ghee
2 onions, sliced
½ kilo (1 lb.) French or other green beans, sliced

salt and pepper
1 teaspoon garam masala

Wash the meat and cut in pieces. Heat the ghee and fry the meat till nicely browned. Fry the onion till golden and add the beans. Fry them gently for a few minutes then spread over the meat in a deeper pan. Sprinkle with salt and pepper and the garam masala. Add a little water and allow to stew till the meat is tender. Serve with bread or rice.

Mutton Stew with Cucumbers
(*Khīra mhāns*)

Make a stew as above with mutton or beef. Place on top of the meat some sliced cucumbers and tomatoes. Season and cook as above. Five minutes before serving sprinkle on tamarind water or lemon juice.

Mutton and Dal Curry

1 cup lentils or dal
salt
½ tablespoon coriander seed
½ teaspoon cumin seed
10 peppercorns
2 red chillies
4 cloves garlic

3 cm. (1 inch) piece ginger, chopped
1 teaspoon turmeric powder
ghee
1 onion, sliced
½ kilo (1 lb.) mutton, cut in cubes

Boil the dal in three cups of salted water till soft. Grind the spices to form a paste. Heat the ghee and fry the onion till golden then add the masala paste and fry for two minutes. Put in the meat and fry till nicely browned. Add the cooked dal and simmer gently till the meat is tender, adding more water if necessary. Serve with rice and yogurt.

Maharashtra Mutton Chops

4 mutton chops
salt
1 teaspoon garam masala
3 cm. (1 inch) piece ginger
6 cloves garlic
1 teaspoon chilli powder or paprika

½ teaspoon cumin seed
ghee for deep frying
½ kilo (1 lb.) potatoes
2 eggs

Wash the chops and boil in a little water with salt to taste and garam masala. Meanwhile grind the ginger, garlic, chilli and cumin seed to make a paste. When the meat is nearly cooked remove from the water and rub the paste well into the chops. Heat 3 tablespoons ghee and nicely brown the chops. Meanwhile boil the potatoes, peel and mash. Cover each chop with potato, beat the eggs and roll well in the egg.

The beaten egg can be applied before covering with potato. Serve with coconut chutney.

Kashmiri Mutton

1 kilo (2 lb.) mutton
4 green cardamoms
5 cm. (2 inch) piece cinnamon, broken
1 tablespoon fennel seed
4 cloves
6 black peppercorns
3 cm. (1 inch) piece ginger
6 cloves garlic

1 teaspoon chilli powder
2 cups curd
½ teaspoon saffron
1 tablespoon lemon juice
4 tablespoons ghee
½ cup almonds, blanched and chopped
½ cup cashew nuts, chopped

Slice the mutton and flatten with a wooden hammer or spoon. Grind together the masala spices and mix well into the curd. Put in the pieces of mutton and allow to marinate. Meanwhile put the saffron in the lemon juice to extract the colour. Cook the marinated mutton gently with a closed lid till the liquid is dried off. Pour over the saffron water, add the ghee and fry the mutton till nicely browned. Fry the nuts till golden and spread over the meat as a garnish. Serve with breads.

Minced Meat Cutlets (*Kīma tikka*)

½ kilo (1 lb.) minced mutton or beef
2 onions, chopped
a few mint leaves, chopped
2 green chillies, sliced
3 cm. (1 inch) piece ginger, finely chopped

salt and pepper
1 egg, beaten
breadcrumbs
ghee

Mix the mince with the onion, mint, chillies and ginger. Add salt and pepper to taste and fold in the egg. Make up the mixture into balls. Roll each ball in the breadcrumbs and form into flat ovals. Heat some ghee for frying and fry the cutlets till nicely browned. Cook gently. Garam masala may be added before cooking if a more spicy taste is required.

Meat Balls (*Kofta*)

Use the same ingredients as for the cutlets in the last recipe. Make the mixture up into balls, roll in flour or gram flour without egg or breadcrumbs.

Meat Ball Curry (*Kofta kari*)

koftas made from ¼ kilo (1 lb.) minced meat
1 tablespoon coriander seeds
1 teaspoon cumin seeds
1 teaspoon turmeric powder
½ teaspoon chilli powder
4 cloves garlic
3 cm. (1 inch) piece ginger
ghee
1 onion, sliced
salt
1 cup coconut milk or creamed coconut

Make the koftas and keep warm. Grind the spices with garlic and ginger to form a paste. Heat the ghee and fry the onion till golden. Add the masala paste and fry for two minutes. Sprinkle with salt to taste and sufficient water to make a gravy. Cook for a further five minutes then pour in the coconut milk. Put in the koftas gently and simmer to heat through so that the koftas do not break up.

Mutton Rolls

¼ kilo (1 lb.) minced mutton or beef
1 tablespoon gram flour
2 tablespoons yogurt
3 cm. (1 inch) piece ginger, finely chopped
2 green chillies, finely sliced
a few chopped coriander leaves
a few chopped mint leaves
1 teaspoon coriander powder
1 teaspoon cumin powder
1 teaspoon garam masala
½ teaspoon paprika or chilli powder
½ teaspoon salt
lemon juice
1 egg, beaten
breadcrumbs
ghee for frying

Mix together the mince with the rest of the ingredients except the egg and breadcrumbs. Add the lemon juice a little at a time and knead well to make small balls. Roll in the egg, then the breadcrumbs, flatten and deep fry in ghee till golden. These variations of koftas can be fried without the egg by rolling in flour. Serve with ginger chutney.

Mutton and Dal Kabab (*Shāmi kabāb*)

½ kilo (1 lb.) minced mutton
2 tablespoons lentils or dal
½ teaspoon cumin powder
½ teaspoon turmeric powder
1 teaspoon coriander powder
salt

2 tablespoons coriander leaves
3 cm. (1 inch) piece ginger
2 green chillies
1 egg, beaten
ghee for frying

Boil the mutton and dal in a little water with the spices and salt to taste. When well cooked and nearly dry keep on one side. Meanwhile grind the coriander leaf with the ginger and chillies. Mix this well with the mince. Now knead in the beaten egg to form a smooth mixture. Make into small balls and fry in ghee till golden. Serve with a fresh chutney and slices of lemon.

Minced Mutton Kabab (*Shīkhampuri kabāb*)

½ kilo (1 lb.) minced mutton
1 teaspoon cumin seeds
1 teaspoon coriander seeds
1 tablespoon gram flour
1 teaspoon poppy seeds
2 tablespoons almonds,
    blanched
4 cloves garlic
ghee

1 onion, sliced
salt
1 egg, beaten
½ cup yogurt
a few mint leaves, chopped
a few coriander leaves, chopped
2 green chillies, finely sliced
1 onion, finely chopped

Boil the mutton in a little salted water till tender. Grind the cumin, coriander, gram flour, poppy seeds and almonds with the garlic to form a paste. Heat the ghee and fry the onion till golden. Add the masala paste and fry for two minutes. Mix in the mutton with salt to taste. Fold in the egg and knead to make a smooth mixture. Form into round flat cakes using some more gram flour. Fry the kababs till golden. Serve with a fresh chutney made with the yogurt, mint and coriander leaves, chillies and chopped onion.

Mutton Kabab (*Bhoti kabāb*)

1 onion, chopped
3 cm. (1 inch) piece ginger
4 cloves garlic
2 green chillies
1 cup yogurt
1 teaspoon garam masala

salt
½ kilo (1 lb.) mutton, cut in
    cubes
ghee
lemon juice

Grind the onion, ginger, garlic and green chillies to a paste. Stir into the yogurt and add garam masala and salt to taste. Marinate the mutton cubes in this mixture for 3–4 hours. Thread the mutton pieces on to skewers and barbecue or put under the grill. Baste with melted ghee and cook slowly till golden. Sprinkle the kababs with a little lemon juice and serve with a fresh chutney and slices of lemon.

Mutton and Egg Kabab (*Nargisi kabāb*)

Ingredients as for Bhoti or Shikhampuri kababs.

4 hard-boiled eggs
2–3 potatoes, par-boiled
2 onions, sliced

4 tomatoes, sliced
cucumber slices

Cook the kababs with rings of egg, potato, onion, tomato and cucumber, taking care not to break the rings. Baste well and serve with chutney and curd or raita.

These kababs come from the Hyderabad region.

Mutton Cutlets

250 g. (½ lb.) minced mutton or
    beef
1 onion, chopped
ghee
1 tablespoon sultanas
1 tablespoon nuts, sliced
3 cm. (1 inch) piece ginger
2 cloves garlic
1 teaspoon cumin seeds
2 green chillies, sliced

2 tablespoons coriander leaf
½ teaspoon turmeric powder
1 teaspoon garam masala
½ kilo (1 lb.) potatoes
1 tablespoon ghee
salt
¼ teaspoon chilli powder
2 eggs, beaten
breadcrumbs

Boil the mince in a little salted water till cooked. Fry the onion in ghee till golden. Add the sultanas and nuts and fry for three minutes. Remove. Meanwhile grind the masala spices and fry for two minutes. Mix together the fried masala, sultanas, nuts and mince. Boil the potatoes, peel and mash. Add salt to taste, ghee and chilli powder. Divide the potato and filling into equal portions and shape the potato round the filling. Dip the cutlets in egg and roll in bread-crumbs. Deep fry till golden. Serve with fresh chutney.

This recipe from Bengal can also be made Maharashtra style by a slight change in the ingredients. Add mint leaves and grated or desiccated coconut to the masala and omit the cumin and turmeric. Add some lemon juice to the filling mixture, otherwise proceed to make your cutlets as above.

Pork

Pork Curry

2 red chillies
1 teaspoon turmeric powder
4 green cardamons
3 cm. (1 inch) piece cinnamon
1 tablespoon coriander seed
3 cm. (1 inch) piece ginger
1 tablespoon coriander leaves

1 kilo (2 lb.) pork, cut in small
  pieces
grated nutmeg
salt and pepper
ghee
1 onion sliced

Grind the masala ingredients. Wash the pork and sprinkle with nutmeg, salt and pepper. Heat the ghee and fry the onion till golden. Add the ground masala and fry for two minutes. Now put in the pork pieces and fry gently till nicely golden. Add a cup of water and continue to cook gently till the pork is tender. Add a little more water if necessary during the cooking. Serve with rice and mango or lemon slices.

Pork Cubes

1 onion, chopped
2 green chillies, sliced
3 cm. (1 inch) piece ginger
4 cloves garlic
1 teaspoon salt
¼ teaspoon chilli powder

1 teaspoon garam masala
1 teaspoon cumin powder
½ kilo (1 lb.) pork, cut in cubes
ghee
lemon juice
chopped fresh coriander leaf

Grind the onion, green chillies, ginger and garlic. Mix in the salt, and spices. Rub this masala well into the pork. Heat a few tablespoons of ghee and gently fry the pork till nicely golden, adding a little water if necessary. Serve sprinkled with lemon juice and coriander leaf.

This recipe is from Coorg, near the Malabar coast. Serve the pork with rice and vegetable.

Pork Vindalu

Here is one of the classic dishes of Western India. Vindalu may be prepared from other meats but pork is the traditional one. The dish is based on the technique of marinating in vinegar and can be made very hot by the liberal use of chilli. The recipe given here is not too hot. Since the meat is virtually pickled it can be kept by as a pickled meat and eaten later hot or cold, as long as the dish is covered either by oil or vinegar.

2 tablespoons coriander seed
1 tablespoon cumin seed
2 green cardamoms
3 cm. (1 inch) piece cinnamon
6 cloves
6 black peppercorns
2 teaspoons turmeric powder
5 cm. (2 inch) piece ginger

½–2 teaspoons chilli powder
1 teaspoon salt
vinegar
1 kilo (2 lb.) pork, cut in cubes
a few bay leaves
ghee
6 cloves garlic
2 teaspoons mustard seed

Lightly roast the coriander and cumin seed in a pan and grind with the rest of the masala ingredients and salt to form a paste, adding a few drops of vinegar. Wash the pork cubes in weak vinegar and cover well with the masala paste, pricking the meat to make sure it is well aromatized. Sprinkle with broken bay leaves and cover with vinegar or wine vinegar. Leave to marinate overnight. Next day heat some ghee and fry the garlic after crushing with a few drops of vinegar. When golden add the mustard seeds and fry till they jump. Now add the pork and its marination liquid and cook gently till the meat is tender. No water should be added to vindalu. Serve hot or cold with rice.

Curd Pork

1 onion, chopped
½ teaspoon turmeric powder
4 black peppercorns
2 cloves garlic
3 green cardamoms
3 cm. (1 inch) piece cinnamon

½ teaspoon salt
1 tablespoon brown sugar
1 cup yogurt
½ kilo (1 lb.) pork, cut in pieces
ghee
lemon juice

Grind the onion with the spices, salt and sugar and beat into the yogurt. Now put in the pork pieces and leave to marinate for 3–4 hours. Heat the ghee and fry the pork and marination paste gently till the meat is tender, adding a little water if necessary. Before serving, sprinkle on lemon juice and serve with plain rice.

Pork Chasnidarh

Chasnidarh is a sweet-and-sour style of cooking where the meat or vegetables are steeped and cooked in a special *chasni* (syrup). It is the combination of spices and aromatics in the chasni and masala that determines the subtlety of your particular dish.

3 tablespoons ghee
2 onions, sliced
4 cloves
4 green cardamons
3 cm. (1 inch) piece cinnamon
3 cloves garlic, finely chopped
½ kilo (1 lb.) pork, cut in pieces
1 teaspoon salt
½ cup lemon juice or vinegar
½ cup brown sugar
1 tablespoon cornflour

1 teaspoon fennel seed, or aniseed
½ teaspoon black pepper
a few curry leaves
¼ teaspoon saffron, dissolved in lemon juice
cucumber slices
chopped celery
tomato slices
½ cup nuts, finely chopped

Heat the ghee and fry the onions till golden. Add the spices and garlic and fry for two minutes. Put in the pork pieces, sprinkle with salt and fry gently till the pork begins to turn golden. Take off the heat. Now make up the chasni. Dissolve the sugar in the acid. Mix the cornflour with a little warm water and add to the sugar and acid. Stir in the fennel or aniseed after crushing, pepper, curry leaves, and saffron water. Steep the pork and vegetable slices in the chasni. Leave for a little while and then heat the whole dish through, making sure that the pork is tender. Serve, sprinkled with the nuts, with plain rice.

Pork Kofta

½ kilo (1 lb.) minced pork or other meat
1 onion, finely chopped

½ teaspoon salt
gram flour
ghee

1 teaspoon cumin powder

½ teaspoon paprika or chilli powder

chasni (see above recipe)

2 teaspoons rosewater

Mix the mince well with the onion, cumin, paprika and salt, form into balls and roll in gram flour. Fry well in ghee and keep aside. Make a chasni as in the above recipe. Steep the koftas in the chasni. Now warm the whole dish gently, sprinkling on the rosewater, till the koftas are heated through.

Liver and Kidney

Fried Liver

3 tablespoons ghee
¼ kilo (1 lb.) liver
salt and pepper
2 onions, sliced

3 cm. (1 inch) piece ginger,
   finely chopped
2 green chillies, sliced

Heat the ghee and first fry the liver, sprinkled with salt and pepper. Now fry the onion, ginger and chillies. Mix with the liver and add a little water to make a gravy. Cook gently till a good gravy is made. Serve with rice and dal.

Liver and Heart Curry

1 kilo (2 lb.) liver and heart
salt
ghee
2 green chillies
2 cloves garlic, finely sliced
3 cm. (1 inch) piece ginger,
   finely chopped

1 red chilli
1 teaspoon cumin seeds
1 teaspoon turmeric powder
4 peppercorns
4 cloves
4 green cardamoms
3 cm. (1 inch) piece cinnamon

Wash the liver and heart and boil in a little salted water till tender. Keep the broth. Slice the cooked meat finely. Heat some ghee and fry the cut masala for two minutes. Meanwhile grind the dry masala and add both masalas to the pan with the chopped meat. Fry for two minutes. Add the broth and simmer gently till a nice gravy is formed. Serve with rice or bread.

Liver Kabab

¼ kilo (1 lb.) liver
ghee
6 cloves garlic
3 cm. (1 inch) piece ginger

1 cup yogurt
1 teaspoon garam masala
1 teaspoon cumin powder
1 teaspoon coriander powder

Boil the liver in a little water till nearly tender. Cut into good-sized cubes and lightly fry in ghee. Grind the garlic and ginger and beat into the curd with the spices. Steep the liver pieces in the curd paste. Fix on to barbecue skewers and gently barbecue or crisp under the grill. Serve with onion rings, lemon slices and tomato. These kababs are made in Hyderabad, central India.

Kidney Curry

½ kilo (1 lb.) lamb or beef
  kidney
vinegar
1 teaspoon poppy seeds
1 teaspoon mustard seed
1 teaspoon cumin powder
1 teaspoon turmeric powder

¼ teaspoon chilli powder
ghee
1 onion, sliced
2 tomatoes, chopped
a few bay leaves
salt

Wash the kidneys and leave to stand in weak vinegar for a few hours. Mix the spices and halve the kidneys. Heat the ghee and fry the onion till golden. Now add the masala mixture and fry for two minutes. Put in the kidneys, tomatoes and bay leaves, sprinkle with salt to taste and fry well. Add a little water and cook gently till the kidneys are tender. Serve with plain rice and dal.

Poultry and Game

Chicken Curry

1 teaspoon turmeric powder
1 teaspoon poppy seed
1 teaspoon cumin seed
6 peppercorns
1 tablespoon coriander seed
3 cloves garlic
3 cm. (1 inch) piece ginger
2 green chillies
3 tablespoons grated or
  desiccated coconut

3 tablespoons ghee
1 onion, chopped
1 chicken, cut in pieces
1 teaspoon salt
1 teaspoon garam masala
juice of a lemon or equivalent
  tamarind water

Grind the spices with the garlic, ginger, chillies and coconut. Heat the
ghee and fry the onion till golden. Add the masala paste. Fry the masala paste for two minutes. Now put in the chicken pieces and fry well.
Add a cup of water, salt and garam masala and simmer gently till the
chicken is tender. Add the lemon juice and serve with rice and dal.

Dry Chicken Curry

2 red chillies
1 tablespoon coriander seed
½ teaspoon fenugreek seed
1 tablespoon cumin seed
1 teaspoon turmeric powder
3 tablespoons ghee
1 onion, sliced

1 teaspoon mustard seed
1 chicken, cut in pieces
a few curry leaves
2 tablespoons grated or
  desiccated coconut
½ cup tamarind water

Grind the masala ingredients. Heat the ghee and fry the onion till golden. Add the mustard seeds and chicken pieces, curry leaves and coconut and fry till the chicken is nicely golden. Add the tamarind water and cook gently till the chicken is tender and the liquid is driven off. Serve with rice and dal or bread with curd.

Fowl Curry

2 tablespoons coriander seeds
1½ teaspoons turmeric powder
1 teaspoon cumin seeds
6 peppercorns
2 red chillies
3 cm. (1 inch) piece ginger
3 cloves garlic
1 tablespoon almonds,
  blanched

ghee
1 onion, sliced
1 tablespoon sultanas
1 chicken or fowl, cut in pieces
salt
3 tablespoons grated or
  desiccated coconut
juice of ½ lemon

Grind the spices, ginger, garlic and almonds together. Warm some ghee and fry the onion till golden. Add the ground masala and sultanas and fry for two minutes. Add the fowl pieces and fry for a further four minutes. Pour in two cups of warm water, salt to taste, coconut and lemon juice, cover and simmer till the meat is tender. Serve with rice.

Chicken Bafat

8 cloves garlic
3 cm. (1 inch) piece ginger
1 teaspoon cumin seed

1 onion, sliced
1 chicken, cut in pieces
1 teaspoon salt

½ teaspoon turmeric powder
2 teaspoons sesame or poppy
  seed
2 teaspoons dal or gram
2 red chillies
½ cup grated or desiccated
  coconut
ghee

4–6 potatoes, par-cooked
4–6 carrots, par-cooked
½ cup tamarind water
1 tablespoon brown sugar or
  grated jaggery
4–6 tomatoes, chopped
½ cup peas

Grind the spices with the coconut to make a paste. Heat some ghee and fry the onion till golden. Add the masala paste and fry for a few minutes. Now put in the chicken pieces and fry till nicely browned. Add a cup of water and salt and simmer gently till the chicken is nearly cooked. Put in the potatoes and carrots, cut in pieces, add the tamarind water and brown sugar. When the sugar has dissolved, put in the tomatoes and peas. Cook the whole together till the meat and vegetables are tender. This Parsi dish goes well with rice and a vegetable curry.

Madurai Chicken

This dish is named after the lovely city of Madura in South India. It can be cooked as a korma or tanduri style.

4 green cardamoms
2 teaspoons sesame or poppy
  seed
2 teaspoons cumin seed
3 cm. (1 inch) piece ginger
2 tablespoons cashew nuts
1 cup yogurt

1 chicken, cut in pieces
tanduri powder (see under
  Spices)
salt
chilli or paprika powder
ghee

Grind the cardamom, sesame seed, cumin seed and ginger with a little water to make a paste. Crush the cashew nuts and blend with the masala paste. Beat the paste into the yogurt. Wash the chicken pieces well and prick the flesh. Rub in enough tanduri powder, salt and paprika or chilli to cover well. Soak the pieces in the spiced curd and leave to stand for a few hours. Heat some ghee and fry the chicken till nicely browned, continue to simmer, adding a little water if necessary, till the meat is tender. The dish should be as dry as possible. Serve with slices of raw onion and lemon and some plain rice.

Roast Masala Chicken

1 teaspoon poppy seed
1 tablespoon gram dal
1 teaspoon cumin seed
4 green cardamoms
5 cm. (2 inch) piece cinnamon
2–4 green chillies
1 tablespoon grated or desiccated
  coconut
2 cloves garlic
3 cm. (1 inch) piece ginger
2 tablespoons ghee

2 onions, sliced
2 tablespoons sultanas
2 tablespoons almonds,
  blanched and chopped
1 tablespoon brown sugar
2 tablespoons chopped
  coriander leaf
a few mint leaves
1 cup yogurt
salt
1 chicken

Grind the masala ingredients with the coconut, garlic and ginger.
Heat the ghee and fry the onion till golden. Add the masala paste and
fry for two minutes. In another pan fry the sultanas and nuts till the
sultanas puff up. Mix in the sugar and fry for another minute. Now
mix the sultanas and sugared nuts with the fried paste. Take from the
heat and add the coriander and mint leaf. Beat into the yogurt and
add salt to taste. Wash the chicken well and prick the flesh all over.
Smear some of the masala curd well into the meat. Put the rest inside
the chicken. Baste well with melted ghee and roast in a moderate oven
till tender.

Spiced Chicken (*Murgh masālam*)

1 tablespoon cumin seed
6 peppercorns
4 green cardamoms
4 cloves
2 green chillies, sliced
4 cloves garlic
3 cm. (1 inch) piece ginger
1 teaspoon salt

2 onions, chopped
2 tablespoons almonds,
  blanched
$\frac{1}{2}$ teaspoon saffron dissolved in
  warm milk
1 chicken, cut in pieces
3 tablespoons ghee

Grind the spices with the garlic, ginger, salt and onions. Grind the
almonds separately with the saffron milk and mix with the masala
paste. Wash the chicken pieces well and prick all over. Cover the
pieces with masala paste and rub well in. Leave to stand for an hour.

Heat the ghee and fry the chicken pieces gently till nicely browned, adding a little water to prevent sticking. Serve with rice or bread.

Fried Chicken

4 green cardamoms
3 cm. (1 inch) piece cinnamon
4 cloves
5 cm. (2 inch) ginger
2 cloves garlic
4 peppercorns
2 teaspoons coriander seed
½ teaspoon chilli powder or paprika

1 chicken, cut in pieces
½ teaspoon turmeric
salt and pepper
3 tablespoons ghee
2 onions, sliced
2 cups coconut milk or creamed coconut

Grind the masala ingredients with a few drops of water to make a paste. Wash the chicken well and prick all over. Rub into the flesh the turmeric, salt and pepper. Heat the ghee and fry the onions till golden. Add the masala paste and fry for two minutes. Put in the chicken pieces and fry well till nicely golden. Pour the coconut milk over them and continue to simmer gently till the meat is tender. Serve with rice.

Hyderabad Chicken

1½ teaspoons turmeric
1 cup yogurt
3 tablespoons ghee
1 onion, sliced
3 cm. (1 inch) piece ginger, finely chopped
6 cloves garlic, finely chopped
2 green chillies, sliced

6 peppercorns
5 cm. (2 inch) piece cinnamon, broken
3 cardamoms
4 cloves
1 chicken, cut in pieces
½ kilo (1 lb.) tomatoes, chopped
salt

Stir the turmeric into the curd. Heat the ghee and fry the onion till golden. Add the rest of the spices and fry for two minutes. Now put in the chicken pieces and fry for a further two minutes. Put in the tomatoes and salt to taste and pour over the curd. Cover and simmer gently till the meat is tender.

Curd Chicken (*Murgh korma*)

1 chicken
lemon juice
yogurt
1 tablespoon coriander powder
1 teaspoon cumin powder
1 teaspoon turmeric powder
½ teaspoon chilli or paprika
  powder
salt
ghee
1 onion, sliced

3 cm. (1 inch) ginger, finely
  chopped
3 cloves garlic, finely chopped
6 green cardamoms
6 cloves
5 cm. (2 inch) piece cinnamon,
  broken
3 tablespoons grated or
  desiccated coconut
chopped fresh coriander leaf

Wash the chicken well and cut in pieces. Wash with weak lemon juice. Fill a bowl with enough yogurt to cover all the chicken pieces. Stir in the powdered spices and salt to taste. Put in the chicken pieces and allow to stand for an hour. Heat the ghee and fry the onion till golden. Add the ginger and garlic and fry for two minutes. Add the cardamoms, cloves and cinnamon and fry for a further two minutes. Put in the chicken pieces and all the yogurt mixture. Fry gently till the yogurt begins to dry up. Add the coconut and more salt if required and enough water to gently cook the meat till tender; 2 teaspoons of poppy seed will help to thicken the gravy. Serve garnished with coriander leaf. If you like the dish hot add more chilli powder.

Chicken Palak

3 tablespoons ghee
2 onions, sliced
4 cloves garlic, finely chopped
3 cm. (1 inch) piece ginger,
  finely chopped
3 cm. (1 inch) piece cinnamon,
  broken

2 teaspoons coriander powder
1 chicken, cut in pieces
4 tomatoes, chopped
2 cups chopped spinach

Heat the ghee and fry the onion till golden. Add the spices and fry for a few minutes. Add the chicken pieces and fry for two more minutes. Put in the tomatoes and spinach, cover and cook gently till the meat is tender.

Chicken Stew

1 chicken, cut in pieces
2 onions, sliced
2 green chillies, sliced
6 tomatoes, chopped
2 tablespoons chopped
    coriander leaf
4–6 potatoes, quartered
6 peppercorns

6 green cardamoms
6 cloves
3 cm. (1 inch) piece cinnamon
a few bay leaves
3 tablespoons ghee
salt
1 cup water

Put the chicken pieces in a pan with all the other ingredients and fry with the ghee for a few minutes. Sprinkle with salt to taste and pour in the water. Stew till the chicken is tender adding more water if necessary.

Peshawari Chicken

Peshawar is near the border with Afghanistan in Pathan country. Here the rugged people have to survive ice-cold mountainous winds which began their journey in Siberia. Mutton and chicken are favourite items in their Moslem diet.

100 g. (4 oz.) minced mutton
chicken liver and heart,
    chopped
1 teaspoon cumin seed
4 peppercorns
4 cloves
1 teaspoon coriander powder
3 cm. (1 inch) piece ginger,
    finely chopped

1 onion, sliced
ghee
salt
½ cup rice
½ cup almonds, blanched and
    chopped
½ cup sultanas
1 chicken
4 cups wholewheat flour (ata)

Boil the mutton mince and heart and liver from the chicken with the spices and onion in two cups of water. Drain the broth when the meat is tender and keep aside. Lightly fry the meat in a little ghee, adding salt to taste. Heat some more ghee in another pan and fry the rice till the grains become opaque. Put in the nuts and sultanas and fry till the sultanas puff up. Pour in the meat broth, or enough liquid to make one cupful, and cook the rice till tender. Now mix in the meat to make a nice stuffing. Put inside the chicken and close up. Make a dough with the flour and water and completely wrap the chicken in this. Put in a greased baking tin and cook in the oven on a low heat. Take off the pastry before serving. If the chicken is wrapped in foil or simply baked and basted, the result will be different. In this part of the country, the chicken may be also coated in clay and baked in the fire like tanduri cooking.

Chicken Vindalu

Some vindalus are quite elaborate in their preparation. Here is a simple but effective recipe for chicken.

1 chicken, cut in pieces	4 cloves garlic
1 teaspoon turmeric powder	2 teaspoons cumin seed
½ teaspoon chilli powder	2 red chillies
1 teaspoon salt	1 tablespoon brown sugar
vinegar	ghee

Wash the chicken pieces well and marinate in a liquid made by dissolving turmeric, chilli powder and salt in a cup of water. Add a cup of vinegar and mix well. Leave for a number of hours or boil together straight away if time is pressing. Grind the garlic, cumin and chillies. Heat some ghee and fry the ground masala for two minutes. Add the chicken and vinegar water and brown sugar. Simmer till the gravy thickens and the meat is tender.

Chicken Moli

1 chicken, cut in pieces	2 tablespoons mustard seed
ghee	3 cm. (1 inch) piece ginger
2 onions, sliced	4 cloves garlic
4 peppercorns	½ teaspoon fenugreek seeds
1 teaspoon salt	1 onion, sliced
1 teaspoon cumin seed	½ cup coconut milk or creamed
1 teaspoon poppy seed	coconut
1 teaspoon turmeric powder	1 tablespoon vinegar
2 red chillies	

Wash the chicken well and heat the ghee. Lightly fry the 2 onions and add the chicken pieces. Fry for two minutes. Now boil in water with peppercorns and salt till nearly tender. Meanwhile grind the spices to make a masala paste. Fry another onion in ghee and add the paste. Fry for two minutes then put in the meat and broth, coconut milk and vinegar. Cook gently together till the meat is tender.

Chicken Fugath

1 chicken, cut in pieces
salt
4 tablespoons ghee
2 onions, finely chopped
3 cm. (1 inch) piece ginger, finely chopped
2 cloves garlic, finely chopped

½ teaspoon paprika or chilli powder
1 cabbage, shredded
1 teaspoon salt
½ cup grated or desiccated coconut

Boil the chicken pieces in salted water till tender. Keep the stock. Heat the ghee and lightly fry the onion, ginger, garlic and paprika. Add the washed and shredded cabbage and sprinkle with salt. When nearly cooked, stir in the coconut and continue frying till tender. Add the chicken pieces and broth just before the cabbage is ready and cook the whole dish together. This dish is a very simply cooked chicken with cabbage fugath. Radishes, beans or other firm vegetables could be used in the same way.

Chicken and Carrots (*Gājar murgh*)

1 chicken, cut in pieces
3 tablespoons ghee
2 onions, chopped
4 cloves garlic, finely chopped
3 cm. (1 inch) piece ginger, finely chopped
1 teaspoon turmeric powder
1 tablespoon coriander powder
3 green cardamoms
3 cm. (1 inch) piece cinnamon

1 teaspoon garam masala
½ teaspoon paprika or chilli powder
½ kilo (1 lb.) carrots, finely sliced
2 cups water
salt
2 tablespoons vinegar
4 hard-boiled eggs, sliced

Wash the chicken pieces well, dry and fry in the ghee till nicely browned. Remove and keep aside. Now fry the onions, using more ghee if necessary, till golden. Now add the spices and fry for two minutes. Put in the carrots and fry well. Add the chicken pieces, water, salt to taste and vinegar. Simmer the dish gently till the meat is tender. Serve garnished with the hard-boiled eggs.

Chicken and Marrow (*Gūda murgh*)

Cook the chicken as above. Replace the carrot with cubed marrow and instead of adding water for the gravy, add coconut milk or creamed coconut.

Sultana Chicken (*Kishmish murgh*)

1 chicken, cut in pieces
salt
ghee
½ cup almonds, blanched and
   chopped
½ cup sultanas
2 onions, sliced
2 cloves garlic, finely chopped
2 red chillies

3 cm. (1 inch) piece ginger,
   finely chopped
1 tablespoon tamarind water
   or vinegar
2 tablespoons brown sugar
3–6 potatoes, quartered and par-
   boiled
1 cup peas

Wash the chicken well and sprinkle with salt. Heat some ghee and fry the chicken till nicely browned. Heat some more ghee and fry the nuts and sultanas. Remove and keep aside. Fry the onions, garlic, chillies and ginger till the onions are golden. Put in the chicken pieces and add the tamarind water, sugar, potatoes and peas. Cook the dish gently till the meat is tender.

Chicken with Apricots (*Arū murgh*)

2 cloves garlic
2 green chillies
1 teaspoon cumin seeds
2 onions, sliced

4 tomatoes, chopped
250 g. (½ lb.) apricots, halved
   and stoned
salt

94

ghee   chopped fresh coriander leaf
1 chicken, cut in pieces

Grind the garlic, chillies and cumin seed. Fry the onions in ghee till golden. Put in the chicken pieces and brown nicely. Add the masala paste, tomatoes, apricots and salt to taste and a little water. Simmer gently till the meat is tender. Serve garnished with coriander leaf with rice or breads.

Chicken with Coconut (*Nareal murgh*)

1 chicken
salt
3 cm. (1 inch) piece ginger
4 cloves garlic
1 teaspoon cumin seed
3 cm. (1 inch) piece cinnamon
6 cloves
6 peppercorns

2 green chillies, sliced
2 tablespoons chopped
    coriander leaf
salt
juice of 1 lemon
½ cup grated or desiccated
    coconut
ghee

Sauce masala:
1 tablespoon coriander seed
½ teaspoon cumin seed
3 cardamons
½ teaspoon fennel seed
1 red chilli

2 tablespoons almonds,
    blanched
1 cup yogurt
½ cup coconut milk or creamed
    coconut

Wash the chicken and remove the heart and liver for boiling. Boil them in a little salted water till tender. Chop well and keep aside. Grind the ginger and garlic together, prick the outside of the chicken and rub with the ginger and garlic paste. Grind together cumin seed, cinnamon, cloves, peppercorns and mix with the chopped heart and liver. Mix in the green chilli, coriander leaf, salt to taste, lemon and coconut. Stuff the chicken and seal up. Baste the chicken with ghee and cook in a moderate oven till tender. Meanwhile grind the spices for the sauce with the almonds and beat the curd. Heat some ghee and fry the masala for two minutes then stir into the curd. Heat gently while stirring in the coconut milk. Add salt to taste and pour over the chicken when serving.

Tandūri Chicken (*Tandūri murgh*)

1 onion, chopped
1 tablespoon coriander seed
4 black peppercorns
3 cm. (1 inch) piece ginger
4 green cardamoms
6 cloves

1 teaspoon salt
2 teaspoons paprika or chilli
  powder
2 teaspoons tanduri powder
1 chicken
ghee

Grind the onion with the masala ingredients. Wash and skin the chicken and prick all over. Rub in the masala paste and grill on skewer whole or cut in pieces. Baste well with ghee. Make a sauce by beating finely chopped mint leaf and a little chilli powder into yogurt. Serve the chicken with a light salad, nans and the sauce. Sometimes tanduri meats are first marinated before roasting. Try basting the chicken with a baste of curd with saffron dissolved in it. If you wish to cook 'tanduri' style, an earthenware baking case can be purchased in the West called a 'chicken brick'. Put the chicken in the brick and bake on an open fire or barbecue or in the oven.

Chicken Kabab

Prepare the chicken as above but first stuff the bird with a stuffing made from 250 g. ($\frac{1}{2}$ lb.) minced meat, lightly fried with 2 cloves of garlic and a few mint leaves. Sprinkle with lemon juice and ghee and cook as above.

Masala Chicken Liver

$\frac{1}{2}$ kilo (1 lb.) chicken livers
salt
$\frac{1}{2}$ teaspoon garam masala
$\frac{1}{4}$ teaspoon turmeric powder
ghee
1 onion, sliced

2 cloves
1 green chilli, sliced
$\frac{1}{2}$ teaspoon cumin powder
3 tomatoes, chopped
chopped fresh coriander leaf

Wash the livers and sprinkle with salt, garam masala and turmeric powder. Heat a little ghee and fry the onion till golden. Add the cloves, green chilli and cumin and fry for two minutes. Add the livers and tomato and cook gently till tender. Serve garnished with coriander leaf.

Duck Curry

2 tablespoons coriander seed
2 red chillies
1 teaspoon turmeric powder
½ teaspoon fenugreek seeds
1 teaspoon poppy seed
½ teaspoon cumin seed
3 cm. (1 inch) piece ginger
3 cloves garlic

3 tablespoons ghee
1 onion, sliced
1 duck, cut in pieces
1–2 teaspoons salt
2 tablespoons grated or
  desiccated coconut
juice of 1 lemon

Grind together the spices, ginger and garlic. Heat the ghee and fry the onion till golden. Add the ground masala and fry for a few minutes. Add the duck pieces and fry for four minutes. Add 2 cups of water, cover and allow to simmer till the meat is tender. Fifteen minutes before serving, add the salt, coconut and lemon juice.

Stewed Duck

2 onions, sliced
ghee
3 cm. (1 inch) piece ginger,
  finely chopped
1 green chilli, sliced
1 teaspoon cumin seed

1 duck, cut in pieces
1 cup peas
1 cup cauliflower pieces
1 cup aubergine cubes
salt and pepper
1 tablespoon vinegar

Fry the onion in a few tablespoons of ghee till golden. Add the ginger, chilli and cumin and fry for two minutes. Add the duck pieces and brown nicely. Now put in the vegetables and enough water to cover the duck and vegetables. Stew gently till the meat is tender and the vegetables are cooked. Before serving adjust seasoning and add the vinegar.

Duck Moli

1 duck, cut in pieces
1 cup coconut milk or creamed
  coconut
2 green chillies
1 teaspoon turmeric powder
1 teaspoon mustard seed
¼ teaspoon cumin seed
2 teaspoons poppy seed
3 cm. (1 inch) piece ginger

3 tablespoons ghee
2 onions, sliced
3–6 potatoes, sliced and par-
  boiled
salt
2 tablespoons vinegar
2 tablespoons grated or
  desiccated coconut

Clean the duck pieces well and boil in coconut milk till tender
Meanwhile grind the masala ingredients. Heat the ghee and fry the
onions till golden. Add the masala and fry for two minutes. Put in
the duck pieces and potatoes, sprinkle with salt and vinegar and pour
on any remaining coconut broth. Cook for five minutes and sprinkle
on the grated coconut. Continue cooking gently till the potato and
duck are well blended in the gravy.

Mango Duck

1 duck, cut in pieces
salt
ghee
2 onions, sliced
2 cloves garlic, finely chopped
3 cm. (1 inch) piece ginger,
  finely chopped

½ teaspoon saffron dissolved
  in lemon juice
2 cloves
3 cm. (1 inch) piece cinnamon,
  broken
½ kilo (1 lb.) mangoes, sliced

Wash the duck and boil in salted water till tender. Keep the stock
aside. Heat the ghee and fry the onions till golden. Add the garlic and
ginger and fry for two minutes. Put in the duck pieces, lemon juice,
cloves, cinnamon and mangoes and duck broth. Continue cooking
gently till the dish is well blended.

Tamarind Duck

3 tablespoons ghee
2 onions, sliced

1 teaspoon turmeric powder
1 duck, cut in pieces

3 green chillies, sliced
3 cm. (1 inch) piece ginger, finely chopped
4 cloves garlic, finely chopped

3 tomatoes, chopped
salt
½ cup tamarind water
chopped fresh coriander leaf

Heat the ghee and fry the onions till golden. Add the spices and fry for two minutes. Put in the duck pieces and fry till nicely brown. Add the tomatoes and salt and a little water and continue cooking gently. When the meat is nearly tender add the tamarind water and cook till the meat is done. Garnish with coriander leaf.

Duck Vindalu

1 duck
vinegar
½ teaspoon cumin seed
8 peppercorns
2 red chillies
2 teaspoons turmeric powder
4 cloves
4 green cardamoms

5 cm. (2 inch) piece cinnamon, broken
salt
3 cm. (1 inch) piece ginger, finely chopped
4 cloves garlic, finely chopped
ghee

Wash the duck well and cut in pieces. Wash the pieces in weak vinegar. Grind the masala ingredients together with a few drops of vinegar to make a paste. Rub the duck pieces well with two thirds of the masala paste and put in a bowl. Sprinkle with salt, ginger and garlic. Pour over vinegar to cover and allow to stand for six hours. Warm a few tablespoons of ghee and fry the rest of the masala. Add to the duck pieces in the bowl. Put in a pot and cook the whole on a slow fire till the duck is tender. The vindalu may be kept in a sterilized jar as long as vinegar or oil covers the meat.

Kashmiri Duck

1 duck
250 g. (½ lb.) minced meat
½ cup pistachio nuts
1 teaspoon cumin seed
½ teaspoon fennel seed
1 tablespoon rosewater

salt
ghee
1 onion, sliced
1 cup yogurt
½ teaspoon turmeric powder
½ teaspoon chilli powder

Wash the duck. Mix together a stuffing of minced meat, nuts, cumin, fennel seed, rosewater and salt to taste. Heat a little ghee and fry the onion till golden. Add the stuffing mixture and fry for a few minutes. Beat the yogurt with turmeric and chilli powder and use to smear the outside of the duck. Put in the stuffing, seal up and baste with the curd and ghee. Bake gently in the oven or barbecue, basting regularly with ghee. Serve with pulau rice.

Roast Goose

Prepare the goose as above but make a stuffing from 250 g. (½ lb.) cooked rice mixed with chopped nuts and fried sultanas. Smear the following mixture on the outside of the goose before baking: 1 tablespoon coriander powder, 1 tablespoon ground fennel seed, ½ teaspoon chilli powder, mixed with lemon juice to make a paste.

Roast Turkey

1 small turkey, cut in pieces	1 teaspoon garam masala
ghee	4 tomatoes, chopped
salt and pepper	salt
1 onion, sliced	2 tablespoons brown sugar
3 cloves garlic, finely chopped	1 green capsicum, finely
3 cm. (1 inch) piece ginger,	chopped
finely chopped	chopped fresh coriander leaf

Put the washed turkey pieces in a baking dish with a little ghee. Sprinkle with salt and pepper and roast gently in the oven. Meanwhile prepare the sauce. Heat some more ghee and fry the onion till golden. Add the garlic, ginger and garam masala and fry for two more minutes. Now add the tomatoes, salt to taste, sugar and capsicum and enough water to cook to form a thick sauce. Serve the roast turkey pieces with the sauce and garnish with chopped coriander leaf.

Rabbit Curry

1 rabbit cut in pieces	ghee
lemon juice	2 onions, sliced

4 black peppercorns
3 cm. (1 inch) piece ginger
4 cloves garlic
½ teaspoon paprika or chilli powder

4 green cardamoms
1 tablespoon mustard seed
a few curry leaves
salt

Wash the rabbit pieces in weak lemon juice. Grind the pepper, ginger, garlic and paprika. Heat some ghee and fry the onions till golden. Add the masala and fry for two minutes. Put in the rabbit pieces and brown nicely. Add the cardamom, mustard seed, curry leaves and salt to taste. Put in enough water for the curry to simmer gently till the meat is tender. Serve with rice and curd.

Fish

Masala Fish

In these recipes the fish is marinated before cooking. The constituents of the marination determine the final taste of the dish. Use any nice filleted fish or fish steaks.

Chilli marination

4 haddock steaks or ½ kilo (1 lb.) fish
1 tablespoon chilli sauce

2 tablespoons vinegar
1 teaspoon salt

Mix together the marination ingredients and soak the washed fish for some hours on both sides. Heat some oil or ghee and fry the fish gently on both sides for a few minutes. Add the marination liquid and cook gently till the fish is ready, turning carefully so as not to break the pieces.

Kashmiri Masāla marination

Use a dessertspoon of Kashmiri masala in place of the chilli sauce.

(See *Essential Spice Recipes* for Kashmiri masala.)

Turmeric marination

Use ½–1 teaspoon turmeric powder in place of the chilli sauce and cook as above.

Baked Masala Fish

1 fish	1 teaspoon garam masala
salt	½ teaspoon chilli powder
1 clove garlic	ghee

Clean a whole fish and rub gently with salted water. Grind the masala ingredients and mix with a little ghee to make a paste. Make small slits in the fish and rub in the paste all over the fish. Baste with oil or melted ghee and wrap in foil. Bake in the oven or fireproof dish without the foil. The masala may be varied by adding your own combinations of spices.

Casserole Masala Fish

1 onion, chopped	2 tablespoons tomato purée
ghee	¼ kilo (1 lb.) fish
2 teaspoons Kashmiri masala	chopped fresh coriander leaf

Fry the onion in ghee till transparent. Add the Kashmiri masala or 2 teaspoons of vindalu paste and fry for two minutes. Add the tomato purée mixed with a little water. Put all in a casserole with the fish and bake with the lid on. When nearly ready garnish with the coriander.

Fish Sambal

1 fish	1 teaspoon cumin seed
salt	1 teaspoon turmeric powder
grated or desiccated coconut	1 clove garlic

green chilli,   sliced curry leaves
1 red chilli   ghee

Clean and prepare the fish and boil in salted water till tender. Remove the skin and mash well, extracting any bones. For every cup of fish have ready ½ cup grated or desiccated coconut, 1 sliced green chilli, and a few curry leaves. Grind the masala with the garlic. Heat the ghee and fry the green chilli and curry leaves for two minutes. Add the ground masala, stir in the fish and fry together. Now add the coconut and simmer the sambal on a slow fire till the coconut is well blended.

Rockfish Sambal

1 red chilli   1 green chilli, sliced
1 teaspoon turmeric powder   3 cm. (1 inch) piece ginger,
1 teaspoon cumin seeds   finely chopped
1 clove garlic   salt
1 fish   a few curry leaves
ghee   ½ cup grated or desiccated
1 onion, sliced   coconut

Grind the chilli, turmeric, cumin and garlic. Wash the fish and boil till tender. Remove the skin and mash. Heat some ghee and fry the onion till golden. Add the masala paste and fry for two minutes. Add the green chilli and ginger. Stir fry and put in the fish, salt and curry leaves and a little water. Cook for a few minutes then put in the coconut and simmer for a further five minutes. A similar sambal may be prepared using prawns.

Fish Moli

In the moli technique of cooking the fish is cooked in coconut as in vindalu the meat is cooked in vinegar.

1 cup coconut milk or creamed   salt
   coconut   ghee
2 teaspoons rice flour or gram   1 teaspoon mustard seed
   flour   2 onions, sliced
1 teaspoon turmeric powder   1 fish
2 cloves garlic, crushed   lemon juice
1 green chilli, finely sliced

Into the coconut milk stir the rice flour, turmeric, garlic, chilli and salt to taste. Heat the ghee and fry the mustard seed for one minute. Now add the onions and fry till opaque. Stir this into the moli liquid and put in the fish which has been carefully washed. Simmer gently till the fish is tender, adding a few drops of lemon juice before serving.

Fish Curry

½ kilo (1 lb.) fresh fish
salt
2 tablespoons ghee
1 onion, sliced
2 cloves garlic, finely chopped
3 cm. (1 inch) piece ginger,
    finely chopped

2 teaspoons coriander powder
1 teaspoon cumin powder
1 teaspoon turmeric powder
½ teaspoon paprika or chilli
    powder
4 tomatoes, chopped
a few bay leaves

Wash the fish and wipe with salted water. Heat the ghee and fry the onion till golden. Add the masala spices and fry for two minutes. Put in the fish, tomatoes and bay leaves and enough water to lightly cook the fish. Sprinkle salt to taste.

Fish with Nuts

1 kilo (2 lb.) white fish
salt
chilli powder
coriander powder
lemon juice
1 red chilli
2 tablespoons cashew nuts
2 tablespoons almonds,
    blanched
1 tablespoon grated or
    desiccated coconut

4 cloves
3 cm. (1 inch) piece ginger
1 tablespoon poppy seed
ghee
2 onions, sliced
salt
a few bay leaves
2 tablespoons pistachio nuts,
    sliced

Wash the fish, make slits in the flesh and rub with a paste of salt, chilli powder, coriander powder and lemon juice. Grind the red chilli, nuts, coconut, cloves, ginger and poppy seed. Heat some ghee and fry the onions till golden. Add the masala paste and fry for two minutes. Put in the fish, sprinkle with salt and a few bay leaves and cover with just enough water to poach lightly till tender. Serve garnished with pistachio nuts.

Baked Fish

1 kilo (2 lb.) fish	1 teaspoon cumin seed
salt	1 teaspoon fenugreek seed
chilli powder	1 teaspoon turmeric powder
vinegar	2 tablespoons ghee
2 cloves garlic	1 cup yogurt
3 cm. (1 inch) piece ginger	sliced lemon
1 tablespoon coriander seed	

Wash the fish and sprinkle with salt, chilli powder and a few drops of vinegar. Bake in a hot oven or grill till the moisture has evaporated. Meanwhile make a sauce by grinding the garlic and ginger with the rest of the spices. Heat the ghee and fry the masala paste for two minutes. Beat this into the yogurt and heat the sauce gently till well blended. Pour over the fish and continue baking till the fish is tender. Serve with slices of lemon.

Sardine Curry

Sometimes it is handy to be able to open a tin of fish and still make a nice curry. Here is one which uses a tin or two of sardines.

2 tablespoons ghee	½ teaspoon chilli powder or paprika
1 onion, sliced	
3 cm. (1 inch) piece ginger, finely chopped	½ cup coconut milk or creamed coconut
2 cloves garlic, finely chopped	tomato purée or chopped tomatoes
1 tablespoon coriander powder	
1 teaspoon cumin powder	salt
½ teaspoon turmeric powder	sardines

Heat the ghee and fry the onion till golden. Add the masala spices and fry for two minutes. Put in the coconut milk, tomatoes to taste and salt. Lastly add the sardines with their oil and cook gently till the dish is well blended.

Saffron Fish

Clean the fish and wash. Grind some saffron with a little salt and a few drops of water to make a paste. Rub the fish well with this mixture and fry gently in ghee.

Fish Pie

cold boiled or fried fish	1 green chilli, finely chopped
breadcrumbs or cooked potato	3 cm. (1 inch) piece ginger, finely chopped
salt and pepper	1 egg, beaten

Mash the fish with the breadcrumbs or some cold cooked potato. Season with salt and pepper, green chilli and ginger. Mix in some of the beaten egg. Fill a baking dish with the fish mixture, spread beaten egg on the top and bake in the oven or grill.

Stuffed Fish

1 whole fish	1 teaspoon turmeric powder
2 onions, finely chopped	1 teaspoon cumin powder
2 tablespoons chopped fresh coriander leaf	ghee
1 green chilli, sliced	salt
2 cloves garlic, finely chopped	tamarind water
3 cm. (1 inch) piece ginger, finely chopped	

Wash the fish and cut open the back. Mix the masala ingredients with the onions. Heat some ghee and fry the mixture for a few minutes. Add salt to taste and tamarind water to make a nice paste. Stuff the paste into the back of the fish and tie up. Baste with ghee and bake in the oven or turn on a spit or barbecue.

Grilled Fish

This is like stuffed fish except that the outside of the flesh is also basted with an aromatic paste.

1 whole fish

For the paste:

½ teaspoon chilli powder or
   paprika
1 tablespoon coriander
   powder
salt
1 cup yogurt
lemon juice

For the stuffing:

4 green cardamoms
2 black peppercorns
1 teaspoon fennel or aniseed
a few mint leaves
2 cloves garlic
ghee
2 onions, sliced
2 tablespoons sultanas
2 tablespoons cashew nuts

Wash the fish well and cut open the back. Make slits in the flesh and make a paste. Beat in the ingredients with the yogurt, adding a little lemon juice. Rub the paste all over the fish. Now grind the stuffing spices. Heat the ghee and fry the onions till golden. Now add the sultanas and nuts and fry till the sultanas puff up. Add the stuffing spices and fry for a few more minutes. Put into the fish and tie up. Bake in the oven or on the spit as above.

Madras Fish Curry

½ teaspoon cumin seed
½ teaspoon poppy seed
½ teaspoon mustard seed
1 red chilli
4 cloves garlic
1 teaspoon turmeric powder

½ kilo (1 lb.) white fish
1 onion, sliced
½ cup tamarind water
salt
ghee

Grind the masala ingredients. Wash the fish well, slice and place in a pan with the onion and tamarind water. Sprinkle with the ground masala and salt to taste. Add two tablespoons of ghee and cook gently till the fish is tender.

Coconut Fish Curry

½ kilo (1 lb.) white fish
ghee
creamed coconut
vinegar

1 teaspoon rice flour
1 teaspoon coriander powder
1 teaspoon turmeric powder
1 onion, sliced

Wash the fish, dry and fry in ghee till golden. Leave to cool. Make half a cup of thick coconut milk by adding warm vinegar to creamed coconut. Make another half-cup of thinner milk and stir in the rice flour, coriander and turmeric. Heat another tablespoon of ghee and fry the onion till golden. Pour in the thin coconut milk and stir well till it thickens. Now carefully add the fish and pour on the thick coconut milk. Cook gently till the dish is well blended.

Tanduri Fish

1 large haddock or red mullet (½ kilo–1 kilo)
1 teaspoon paprika or tanduri powder
4 tablespoons coriander seed
1 teaspoon salt
6 cardamoms
1 onion, chopped
2 cloves garlic
6 peppercorns
2 teaspoons fennel or aniseed
2 tablespoons chopped fresh mint leaf
1 cup yogurt
juice of 1 lemon

Wash the fish and dry. Grind all the marination ingredients and beat into the yogurt, adding the lemon juice. Make slits in the fish and rub the paste in well. Leave the fish to stand for at least an hour. The longer the marination, the more aromatic will the fish become. Cook on a spit, grill or charcoal barbecue or bake in a 'fish brick', the nearest thing to a tandur which can be purchased in the West. Cook gently till tender inside and crisp on the outside, basting with ghee if necessary.

There are many variations of the tanduri paste and here your flair for experimentation can be used. To the same amount of yogurt, grind these ingredients and add:

3 cm. (1 inch) piece ginger
6 cloves
6 cardamoms
1 teaspoon cumin seeds
1 onion, chopped
1 red chilli
salt

The fish may also be marinated in lemon juice or tamarind juice mixed with herbs and spices before tanduri-style cooking.

Fish Sorak

½ kilo (1 lb.) fish
salt and pepper
ghee
2 red chillies
1 clove garlic
¼ teaspoon cumin seed

3 cm. (1 inch) piece ginger
1 teaspoon turmeric powder
1 cup coconut milk or creamed
  coconut
½ green mango or 1 sliced
  lemon

Wash the fish, dry and sprinkle with salt and pepper and cut in slices. Heat some ghee and fry the fish gently. Meanwhile grind the spices. Mix with the coconut milk, put in a pan and add the fried fish and mango slices. Simmer uncovered for fifteen minutes.

Salt Fish Curry with Tomatoes

2–3 slices salt fish
ghee
½ teaspoon cumin seeds
1 teaspoon turmeric powder
4–6 cloves garlic
3 cm. (1 inch) piece ginger

1 red chilli
small bunch spring onions,
  chopped
½ kilo (1 lb.) tomatoes, chopped
tamarind or lemon juice

Steep the fish in water for half an hour or longer if very salty. Meanwhile grind the masala ingredients. Heat some ghee and fry the onions for two minutes. Add the ground masala and fry for a further two minutes. Add the tomatoes and fry well. Cut the fish into small pieces and add to the frying tomatoes. Cover and simmer till the fish is cooked. Now add a tablespoon of tamarind or lemon juice. More gravy can be made by adding half a cup of water or coconut milk.

Salt Fish and Mixed Vegetables

salt fish
3 carrots, sliced
3 potatoes, chopped
1 aubergine, sliced
2 onions, sliced
½ teaspoon cumin seed
1 teaspoon turmeric powder

4–6 cloves garlic
3 cm. (1 inch) piece ginger
2 red chillies
½ cup coconut milk or
  creamed coconut
1 tablespoon ghee

Cut the soaked fish in pieces and put in a pan with the vegetables and one of the onions. Grind the masala and sprinkle over. Pour on the coconut milk and simmer till the fish is soft, adding more water if necessary to cook the vegetables. Heat ghee and fry the second onion, then add the curry and fry to taste.

Sindhi Fish Cutlet

1 white fish
1 onion, chopped
2 green chillies, sliced
3 cm. (1 inch) piece ginger, finely chopped
1 tablespoon chopped fresh coriander leaf

a few mint leaves, chopped
½ teaspoon turmeric powder
½ teaspoon garam masala
1 teaspoon cumin seeds
salt
2 eggs, beaten
ghee

Wash the fish and boil till tender in a little salted water. Meanwhile mix the ingredients for the stuffing. Mash the cooked fish and mix well with the cumin seed and salt. Form into balls and make a depression in the middle of each. Put in some of the stuffing mixture and roll up. Flatten to form cutlets and moisten with beaten egg. Shallow fry in ghee till golden. Serve with a chutney.

Fish Kabab

1 kilo (2 lb.) fish steaks
lemon juice
1 teaspoon cumin powder
½ teaspoon chilli powder or paprika

salt
1 teaspoon garam masala
1 cup yogurt
2 onions, sliced in rounds
ghee

Wash the fish and cut in pieces to barbecue on the skewer. Smear with lemon juice. Beat the cumin, chilli powder, salt and garam masala into the yogurt. Put the fish pieces in the yogurt paste, cover all over and leave to marinate for an hour. Put on skewers with onion rounds, baste well with ghee and cook gently till tender. This dish may also be prepared by cooking under the grill or even baking in the oven.

Goan Fish Cutlet

½ kilo (1 lb.) white fish
ghee
1 onion, finely chopped
3 cm. (1 inch) piece ginger,
  finely chopped
2 green chillies, sliced
½ teaspoon turmeric powder
1 teaspoon cumin seed

4 tomatoes, chopped
a few mint leaves
2 cloves
small piece cinnamon
salt
chopped fresh coriander leaf
2 eggs, beaten

Wash the fish and boil in a little water till tender. Heat the ghee and fry the onion till golden. Add the ginger, chillies, turmeric and cumin seed and fry for two minutes. Put in the tomatoes, mint, cloves, cinnamon, salt and some coriander leaf. Stir in the flaked cooked fish and fry well. Remove from the heat and make up the mixture into cutlets. Roll in the beaten egg and fry till golden. Serve with fresh chutney.

Fish Pakodas

Pakodas are very popular in Sind. In other parts of India they are known as pakoras, as well as other names. The batter is made from gram flour. Here is a spicy batter for use with fish.

1 cup gram flour (besan)
1 teaspoon cumin powder
½ teaspoon chilli powder or
  paprika
1 teaspoon coriander powder
a few mint leaves, finely
  chopped

small piece ginger, finely
  chopped
½ teaspoon bicarbonate of soda
salt
fish fillets

Add water to the flour to make a creamy batter. Beat in the rest of the ingredients with salt to taste. Leave the batter to stand. Boil or steam the fillets till tender. Cut into pieces and dip in the pakoda batter. Deep fry in ghee till nicely golden.

Shellfish

Prawn Rice

2 cups rice
ghee
2 onions, sliced
4 cloves garlic, finely chopped
2 green chillies, sliced
½ teaspoon cumin powder

salt
2–4 tomatoes, chopped
2 tablespoons chopped fresh
    coriander leaf
1 cup prawns
½ cup tamarind water

Wash the rice and boil in four cups of water or enough water to cook till tender. Heat some ghee and fry the onions till golden. Add the garlic, chillies, cumin and salt to taste and fry for two minutes. Put in the tomatoes and coriander leaf and simmer gently. Heat some ghee in another pan and lightly fry the washed prawns for two minutes. Add the tamarind water and cook gently for two more minutes. Pour in the fried masala. When well blended, mix with the cooked rice and serve with Parsi Green Curry.

Prawns and Greens

¼ kilo (1 lb.) green-leaved
    vegetable

3 cm. (1 inch) piece ginger,
    finely chopped

ghee

2 green chillies, sliced

1 onion, sliced

1 cup small prawns

2 cloves garlic, sliced

salt

Wash and drain the green leaves and chop coarsely. Heat some ghee and fry the onion till golden. Add the greens a little at a time with the garlic, ginger and green chillies. When the baji is half cooked, put in the prawns and simmer till the prawns and greens are cooked. Sprinkle with salt to taste.

Deep-fry Prawns

3 cm. (1 inch) piece ginger

½ teaspoon chilli powder

4 cloves garlic

lemon juice

½ teaspoon turmeric powder

250 g. (½ lb.) big prawns

½ teaspoon garam masala

rice flour or gram flour

salt

ghee or oil

Grind the ingredients with lemon juice to form a paste. Roll the washed and shelled prawns in the paste and leave to marinate for half an hour. Roll again in the flour and deep fry. Serve with fresh chutney.

Prawn Bhajia

Maharashtra has a beautiful sea coast and the country is famous for its fish and shellfish recipes. Here is one for prawns in batter.

1 cup gram flour (besan)

1 green chilli, sliced

½ teaspoon turmeric powder

½ teaspoon bicarbonate of soda

½ teaspoon garam masala

1 tablespoon grated or

1 onion, finely chopped

    desiccated coconut

3 cm. (1 inch) piece ginger,

salt

    finely chopped

1–2 cups prawns

a few curry leaves

ghee or oil

½ teaspoon chilli powder or

    paprika

Add enough water to the gram flour to make a creamy batter. Beat in the rest of the ingredients with salt to taste. Dip the washed prawns in the batter and deep fry till golden. Serve with chutney.

Prawn Curry

ghee
1 onion, sliced
1 tablespoon coriander powder
½ teaspoon chilli powder or
  paprika
1 teaspoon turmeric powder
1 teaspoon poppy seed
½ teaspoon cumin seed
3 cm. (1 inch) piece ginger,
  finely chopped
2 cloves garlic, finely chopped
1 cup shelled prawns
½ cup coconut milk or creamed
  coconut
lemon juice

Heat some ghee and fry the onion till golden. Add the masala spices and fry for two minutes. Put in the prawns and fry for a few more minutes. Add the coconut milk and acidulate with the lemon juice to taste. This curry is nice with potatoes and pumpkin or marrow added.

Prawn Pakodas

Make a batter as for Fish Pakodas and deep fry the prawns. Sprinkle with tamarind water or lemon juice and serve with a chutney.

Prawn Cutlets

1 cup prawns
2 tablespoons grated or
  desiccated coconut
1 green chilli, sliced
a few coriander leaves
1 teaspoon turmeric powder
½ teaspoon chilli powder
1 teaspoon cumin powder
1 clove garlic, finely chopped
salt
breadcrumbs
ghee

Mash the washed prawns and mix with the coconut, chilli and coriander leaf. Mix the masala ingredients with the garlic and salt to taste and stir into the prawns. Form into cutlets with breadcrumbs and fry in ghee. Serve with chutney.

Lobster Curry

½ kilo (1 lb.) lobster
½ teaspoon cumin seeds
10 peppercorns
1 red chilli
1 teaspoon turmeric powder
4 cloves
4 cardamoms
5 cm. (2 inch) piece cinnamon, broken
4 cloves garlic, sliced
3 cm. (1 inch) piece ginger, sliced
tamarind water
vinegar
ghee
1 onion, sliced
salt

Put the lobster in cold water and boil for ten minutes. Cool and shell, removing the dark vein in the back. Meanwhile grind the masala ingredients. Press out a little tamarind juice for acidulation using vinegar instead of water. Heat some ghee and fry the onion till golden. Add the lobster meat, cut in pieces, and the ground masala, garlic and ginger, and fry for three minutes. Pour in sufficient warm water to make a gravy and simmer till the lobster is tender. Finally add the acid and salt to taste. This recipe can also be used for crabs.

Lobster Patties

lobster
1 onion, sliced
a few mint leaves
1 green chilli, sliced
3 cm. (1 inch) piece ginger, finely chopped
ghee
salt

Remove the lobster meat from the shells and mince. Grind the onion with the rest of the ingredients. Heat a little ghee and fry the onion paste for a few minutes. Add the lobster flesh and salt and fry for a few more minutes. Fill up the shells with the fried lobster and put in the oven to bake for five minutes.

Cockle Curry

1 plate of cockles
½ teaspoon cumin seed
6 peppercorns
1 teaspoon turmeric powder
4 cloves garlic
ghee
1 onion, finely chopped
½ cup tamarind water

1 red chilli
3 cm. (1 inch) piece ginger

½ cup coconut milk or creamed coconut

Open the cockles and wash well. Grind the masala ingredients with the ginger and garlic. Heat some ghee and fry the onion till golden. Add the masala paste and fry for two minutes. Put in the cockles with enough water to make a gravy. Allow to simmer for half an hour, then add the tamarind water and coconut milk and simmer for five more minutes, stirring constantly.

Tales of Deviprasad:
Necessity, the Mother of Invention

Deviprasad had been demonstrating one of the key principles of the great art while the boys watched in silence. All that could be heard was the happy bubbling of water in a shining pot. Subtle aromas filled the air. Then Deviprasad looked up at the group and noticed one boy frowning. He spoke to them softly. 'It is often only when we are forced by circumstances to act faster than reason will allow us that deep and true learning takes place. The son of an ancient master had been pestering his father to reveal his culinary knowledge before he died, for the father was now very old.

'"I know nothing, my son, that has not come to me through experience, but I will reveal my most important secret to you this evening," said the old man.

'"At last!" cried the boy. "I can hardly wait."

'"Stay here, then, and look after the house while I go to transact some important business in the town. I will return this evening. Make sure you have taken your bath and put on fresh clothes."

'Somewhat mystified, the boy assured his father that he would do his bidding. That evening the old man returned in good spirits.

'"Good boy. Now come with me." The old man took his son's hand and soon they found themselves at the back entrance to a large building that glowed like a bowl of pure milk in the moonlight.

'"Now," said the father, "wait in there and tell the first person you meet that you are the new cook." And before the boy had finished his protestations he was pushed smartly through the doorway and a gate slammed shut behind him. A tall bearded man stood in front of him, his expression fiercely critical.

'"I am the new cook," stammered the boy.

'"The new cook? You don't look like one to me. However, if you say you are the new cook, then you must be." The bearded man looked at him with disdain, then continued. "I have an important guest coming later this evening. Here is a list of the dishes I will require. You can read I suppose?"

'"Oh, yes," replied the boy, "but . . . "

'"Good! Make sure they are ready then. You will find everything you need in the next room which is the kitchen. Well, don't stand there gaping at me, you'd better get started hadn't you?"

'"Yes," said the boy, too bewildered to protest any further.

'When the tall man had gone he glanced for the first time at the list of dishes. His heart sank. There were so many of them and each seemed to require some special treatment or mixture of spices. Time was against him. Then, into his mind flashed a picture of his father, smiling and nodding as if he approved of his son's thoughts. Suddenly the boy felt calm. He moved with assurance. He inspected the cupboards and their contents for the ingredients and began arranging them carefully in groups on the big kitchen table. Then a door opened and two servants appeared.

'"Who are you?" one of them asked.

'" I am the new cook and tonight I have been instructed to create a masterpiece."

'The servant looked at his companion, grinned and put a hand to his mouth.

'"Attend to the fire at once!" The boy turned to the other and looked him straight in the eye. "Start preparing these vegetables while I see to the meat. We have no time to waste. Did you hear me?"

'"Yes, sir," replied the servants and they set to work at once. Then one of them stopped and looked at him again.

'"And don't look so astonished. I know you will do your best. Together we shall amaze the master and his guest!"

'"Yes indeed, sir," the servant grinned.

'The boy's heart pounded in his breast. Skilfully he cut the meat, carefully he ground and blended the spices to make the masalas. One by one he found the right mixtures. There was no time for mistakes. One by one the dishes took shape under his discerning eye. The boy tasted nothing; his sense of smell seemed extra sharp. He could tell by the texture and fragrance of each dish whether his methods were correct. Suddenly the door burst open. There stood the bearded master of the house.

'"Well, my new cook, something tells me you have excelled yourself this evening. Let us hope so. My guest is a most critical admirer of the culinary arts. You may sleep here tonight and return to your father's home tomorrow."

'The boy thanked him and then begged the favour of an explanation. The bearded man laughed.

'"Listen to him. No, no, no, my boy, I think you have received quite enough explanations for one evening."

'The following morning, the old man was at his door to greet his son. He put his arms around the boy's shoulders and looked into his eyes. The boy told him all that had happened and how pleased the master of the house had been afterwards. Though he had to admit that the whole affair still seemed a mystery to him, even though very enjoyable.

'"Well, my son, you seem to have learned my secret. And that suggestion of saffron in the third dish – a master stroke!"

'The boy looked at his father for a moment, then they both began to laugh.'

The boys stood in silence, still watching the animated face of their teacher. The shining pot bubbled gently on the fire. A smile slowly spread over the face of the boy who had been frowning. Deviprasad sighed and turned to the pot. . . .

Legumes

In India, the legume family supplies a number of peas and beans which are used fresh or dried. Dried legumes are stored whole or split. When split they are called *dāl*. They are boiled to make a thick sauce which functions in a similar way to the gravy of Western dishes. They are also used in sweets and cutlets. Gram flour is used in batters, pancakes and chapatis. The legumes are rich in protein and any legume dish will provide really nourishing food.

Red Lentils (*Masūr dāl*)

1 cup red lentils
1 teaspoon salt
1 teaspoon cumin seeds
1 teaspoon poppy seeds
1 teaspoon paprika or chilli powder
1 teaspoon turmeric powder
2 teaspoons coriander seeds
6 cloves

5 cm. (2 inch) piece cinnamon
4 green cardamoms
1 cup grated or desiccated coconut
4 black peppercorns
4 cloves garlic
2 tablespoons ghee
2 onions, chopped

Wash the dal and leave to soak for an hour. Drain and bring to the boil with salt in a little water. Cook on a medium heat. Meanwhile grind all the ingredients except the onion. Heat the ghee and fry the onion till golden. Add the masala paste and fry for a few minutes. Stir into the dal just before it is ready. Serve hot with rice and curry.

Split Green Peas (Mūng dāl)

1 cup mung dal
1 teaspoon salt
½ teaspoon turmeric powder
2 tablespoons ghee
2 onions, chopped
2 cloves garlic, finely chopped

3 cm. (1 inch) piece ginger, finely chopped
½ teaspoon cumin seeds
1 teaspoon coriander powder
chopped coriander leaf

Wash the dal and leave to soak for an hour. Drain and boil in a little water with salt and turmeric till soft. Meanwhile, heat ghee and fry the onion, garlic and ginger till golden. Stir in the cumin and coriander powder and fry for a few minutes. Add to the dal a few minutes before it is ready. Serve hot garnished with the chopped coriander. Serve with a curry and chapatis.

Hot Lentils (Sambhar)

1 cup dal
2 carrots, chopped
2 potatoes, chopped
1½ teaspoons salt
2 teaspoons turmeric powder
½ cup tamarind water or lemon juice
2 tablespoons ghee
1 teaspoon cumin powder

2 teaspoons coriander powder
½ cup grated or desiccated coconut
1½ tablespoons mustard seeds
2 green chillies, chopped (optional)
a few curry leaves
2 teaspoons sambhar masala (See Essential Spice Recipes)

Wash, soak and boil the lentils with carrots, potatoes, salt and turmeric in three cups of water till tender. Meanwhile add the tamarind or lemon juice to the dal. Heat the ghee and fry the cumin, coriander and coconut. Add the mustard seeds, green chilli and curry leaves and fry for a few minutes. Add sambhar masala, mix well and stir into the dal. Serve hot with dosas or boiled rice.

Creamed Lentils (*Mughlai dāl*)

1 cup black gram (urhad dal)
1 teaspoon salt
½ teaspoon turmeric powder
1 green chilli, sliced
3 cm. (1 inch) piece ginger,
   finely chopped
a few bay leaves
2 tomatoes, chopped

½ cup yogurt, beaten
ghee
1 onion, sliced
½ teaspoon chilli powder or
   paprika
½ cup cream or creamy milk
lemon juice

Wash the dal and leave to soak for some hours. Add salt, turmeric green chilli, ginger and bay leaves and simmer till the dal is tender, Add the tomatoes and yogurt and stir well. Meanwhile heat some ghee and fry the onion till golden. Add the chilli powder and fry for two minutes. Stir into the dal with the cream and some lemon juice. Serve with chapatis or nans and chutney.

Split Tuvar Peas (*Tūr dāl*)

In the North of India tur dal is hardly used but in Gujerat the word *dāl* refers to tur dal. Gujerati dishes have a sweet-sour taste which is given by a combination of sugar and lime or lemon. Here is one of the Gujerati dal dishes.

1 cup tur dal
salt
½ teaspoon turmeric powder
1 teaspoon garam masala
½ teaspoon chilli powder or
   paprika
3 tablespoons brown sugar or
   jaggery
2 tablespoons ghee
1 teaspoon mustard seed

1 teaspoon fenugreek seed
a few curry leaves
3 cm. (1 inch) piece ginger,
   finely chopped
1 green chilli, sliced
juice of 1 lemon
2 tablespoons coriander leaves,
   chopped
1 tablespoon grated or
   desiccated coconut

Wash the dal and boil in salted water till soft. Add the turmeric, garam masala, chilli powder, sugar. Heat a little ghee and fry the mustard seeds, fenugreek, curry leaves, ginger and green chilli for a few minutes. Add to the dal with the lemon juice. Sprinkle with coriander leaf and coconut and simmer till the dish is well blended.

Split Green Peas with Spinach (*Mūng dāl palak*)

½ kilo (1 lb.) spinach
1 cup mung dal
salt
2 tablespoons ghee
1 onion, sliced
3 cm. (1 inch) piece ginger, finely chopped

½ teaspoon turmeric powder
½ teaspoon chilli powder or paprika
1 teaspoon cumin seeds

Wash the spinach (palak) and chop. Cook together with the dal in a little salted water till the dal is tender. Heat the ghee and fry the onion till golden. Add the rest of the ingredients and stir the whole into the dal. Cook for a few more minutes together till the dish is well blended.

Bengal Peas (*Kabli channa*)

1 cup Kabli channa
salt
3 tablespoons ghee
2 onions, sliced
3 cm. (1 inch) piece ginger, finely chopped
4 tomatoes, chopped

1 teaspoon turmeric powder
1 teaspoon garam masala
½ teaspoon chilli powder or paprika
½ cup tamarind water
1 green chilli, sliced
chopped fresh coriander leaf

Soak the channas for some hours and boil in salted water till tender but not mushy (keep the channas whole). Heat the ghee and fry the onions till golden. Add the ginger, tomatoes, turmeric, garam masala and chilli powder and fry for two minutes. Put in the channas and tamarind water and cook together for a few minutes. Serve sprinkled with the sliced chilli and coriander leaf. These channas are also delicious served dry, sprinkled with a little lemon juice, salt and chilli powder.

Gram Flour Kachoris (*Dāl kachoris*)

½ cup black dal (urhad dal)
2 peppercorns

2 tablespoons ghee
salt

2 teaspoons coriander seeds
½ teaspoon cumin seeds
1 red chilli

4–5 cups wholewheat flour (ata)
milk or yogurt
ghee or oil for deep frying

Soak the dal overnight. Next day grind with the spices. Heat the ghee and fry the dal mixture till tender. Add salt to taste. Make a dough by mixing the flour with milk or yogurt. Knead well and divide into balls. Make a depression in each ball and stuff with the gram mixture. Roll out the kachoris like a stuffed paratha but deep fry like a puri. Serve with chutney.

Medu Vada

Vadas, made from gram flour, are favourite fried savouries in the south. This Medu Vada comes from Tamil Nadu.

1 cup tur dal
salt
1 aubergine, sliced
2 potatoes, chopped
2 tomatoes, chopped
a few curry leaves
ghee
1 onion, sliced
½ teaspoon chilli powder or
   paprika

2 bay leaves
2 cloves
1 teaspoon turmeric powder
1 teaspoon cumin powder
1 teaspoon fenugreek seed
½ cup tamarind water
1 cup urhad dal flour
ghee or oil for deep frying

Make up a tur dal sauce as follows: soak the dal, boil in salted water till tender. Before the dal is soft add the vegetables and curry leaves. Heat some ghee and fry the onion till golden. Add the paprika or chilli powder, bay leaves, cloves, turmeric, cumin, and fenugreek seeds. Fry for a few minutes. Put in with the dal and stir in the tamarind water. Heat gently and keep warm. Make up the vadas by mixing the dal flour with a little water, salt and chilli powder. Make the dough into small balls and form a depression in each. Deep fry the vadas and serve with the tur dal poured over. Vadas are also tasty with sambhar.

Alu Vada

1 cup black dal (urhad dal)
1 green chilli, sliced
3 cm. (1 inch) piece ginger
3-4 potatoes, boiled, peeled and
  mashed
1 tablespoon coriander leaves
salt
ghee or oil for deep frying
½ cup grated or desiccated
  coconut

1 teaspoon cumin seed
1-2 cups yogurt
2 tablespoons fried sultanas
2 tablespoons almonds,
  blanched and sliced
garam masala
lemon juice or tamarind water

Soak the dal for a number of hours, drain and grind with the chilli
and ginger. Add the potato, coriander leaf and salt to taste and knead
well. Make the mixture into small balls and form a depression in the
centre of each. Deep fry the vadas till golden and keep warm. Grind
the coconut with the cumin seed and beat into the yogurt. Add the
sultanas and nuts and put the whole mixture in the depressions in
the vadas. Sprinkle them with garam masala and lemon juice.

Vegetables

Pea and Potato Curry (*Matar batāta kari*)

2 tablespoons ghee
1 onion, sliced
1 tablespoon chopped
  coriander leaf
3 cm. (1 inch) piece ginger,
  finely chopped
1 teaspoon turmeric powder
½ teaspoon cumin powder
1 teaspoon coriander powder

½ teaspoon chilli powder or
  paprika
2 cups peas
½ kilo (1 lb.) potatoes, par-
  boiled, chopped
4 tomatoes, chopped
2 teaspoons salt
1 teaspoon garam masala
1 tablespoon lemon juice

Heat the ghee and fry the onion till golden with the coriander and
ginger. Add the spices and fry for two minutes. Stir in the peas,
potatoes, tomatoes and salt and cook gently till tender. Serve sprinkled with garam masala and lemon juice. Broad beans and other green
beans can be prepared in this way.

Peas and Carrots (*Gājar matar*)

1 tablespoon ghee
½ teaspoon caraway seed
½ kilo (1 lb.) carrots, sliced
½ kilo (1 lb.) peas
½ teaspoon turmeric powder

salt
½ teaspoon coriander powder
½ teaspoon chilli powder or
   paprika
chopped fresh coriander leaf

Heat the ghee and fry the caraway seeds with the carrots and peas. Add the turmeric, salt to taste, coriander and chilli powder. Add a little water and cook till the vegetables are tender. Serve garnished with coriander leaf.

Peach Curry (*Arū ka kari*)

2 tablespoons ghee
1 teaspoon mustard seed
½ cup grated or desiccated
   coconut
1 teaspoon turmeric powder

2 cups peaches, cubed
3 cloves
1 tablespoon brown sugar
1 teaspoon salt
chopped fresh coriander leaf

Heat the ghee and fry the mustard seeds till they jump. Add the coconut, turmeric and fry for a few minutes. Put in the peaches, a little water, cloves, sugar and salt, simmer gently for ten minutes. Serve sprinkled with coriander leaf. Rice and meat curry go well with this peach or apricot dish, especially mutton or lamb.

Mango Curry (*Ām ka kari*)

1 red chilli
½ teaspoon fenugreek seed
1 teaspoon turmeric powder
½ teaspoon cumin seed
3 cm. (1 inch) piece ginger
2 cloves garlic

ghee
½ teaspoon mustard seed
6 green mangoes, halved or
   equivalent weight of plums
salt

Grind the masala ingredients, adding a few drops of water to make a paste. Heat the ghee and fry the mustard seeds till they jump. Stir in the masala paste and fry for three minutes. Add the mangoes or plums with a little water and salt to taste. Simmer gently till the fruit is tender. Serve with meat and rice and curd.

Broccoli in Curd (*Dahi sāg*)

½ kilo (1 lb.) broccoli or similar
  vegetable
2 tablespoons ghee
1 onion, sliced
1 teaspoon chilli powder or
  paprika
1 teaspoon turmeric powder

2 teaspoons coriander powder
2 cardamoms
4 cloves
1 cup yogurt
salt
lemon juice

Wash and soak the broccoli in water. Heat the ghee and fry the onion till golden. Add the masala ingredients and fry for two minutes. Add the broccoli after coarsely chopping, with the yogurt. Sprinkle with salt and lemon juice to taste. Cook gently till the vegetable is tender.

Banana Ball Curry (*Kela kofta kari*)

Wherever bananas or plantains are grown, banana curries are popular.

1 kilo (2 lb.) bananas
gram flour (besan)
ghee for frying
1 onion, finely chopped
3 cm. (1 inch) piece ginger,
  finely chopped
1 green chilli, finely sliced
1 tablespoon sultanas
1 tablespoon mixed nuts,
  finely chopped

lemon juice
For the sauce:
2 onions, chopped
2 cloves garlic
1 tablespoon coriander seeds
½ teaspoon turmeric powder
½ teaspoon fenugreek seeds
¼ cup yogurt
salt
chopped fresh coriander leaf

Chop the bananas and boil in a little water till tender. Mash them and mix with enough gram flour (up to half-kilo) to make a stiff dough. Meanwhile heat some ghee and fry the onion till golden. Add half of the chopped ginger, the green chilli, sultanas, nuts and a little lemon juice and fry for two minutes. Make up the dough into small balls with a depression in the middle. Fill with the remaining sultanas and nut stuffing and roll up. Fry in ghee till golden. Now make up the sauce. Grind the onions with the rest of the ingredients except the yogurt. Heat some more ghee and fry for two minutes. Beat into the curd with salt to taste. Add a little water and cook gently for a few minutes to make a thick gravy. Put in the koftas and heat them well enough. Serve garnished with chopped coriander leaf.

Parsi Green Curry

2 onions, chopped
4 tablespoons grated or
  desiccated coconut
6 cloves garlic
3 cm. (1 inch) piece ginger
2 green chillies
1 tablespoon poppy seed
1 teaspoon cumin seed

1 teaspoon turmeric powder
4 tablespoons chopped fresh
  coriander leaf
2 tablespoons ghee
2 cups coconut milk or creamed
  coconut
salt
1 tablespoon lemon juice

Grind the onions with the masala ingredients to form a paste. Heat the ghee and fry the masala paste for five minutes. Add the coconut milk and salt to taste and simmer gently for ten minutes. Add the lemon juice and serve with prawn rice.

Steamed Potato (*Ālū dam*)

½ kilo (1 lb.) potatoes
1 onion, chopped
3 cm. (1 inch) piece ginger
1 teaspoon coriander seed
3 cm. (1 inch) piece cinnamon
ghee
chilli powder

salt
a few bay leaves
½ teaspoon turmeric powder
½ cup yogurt
garam masala
chopped fresh coriander leaf

Peel the potatoes, prick with a fork and soak in water for an hour. Grind the onion, ginger, coriander seed and cinnamon to make a paste. Heat the ghee. Take out the potatoes and rub with chilli powder. Fry them till golden and keep aside. Now fry the masala paste for two minutes. Add the salt, bay leaves, turmeric powder and beaten curd. Put in the potatoes with a little water, cover and steam gently till the potatoes are tender. Serve sprinkled with garam masala and coriander leaf.

Vegetable balls can be made of any combination of vegetables, mixed with gram flour and fried.

Vegetable Balls (*Sabzi kofta*)

250 g. (½ lb.) potato, celery and
  carrot
1 cup gram flour (besan)
1 teaspoon garam masala
½ teaspoon chilli powder
1 teaspoon salt
ghee or oil for frying

Boil the vegetable till tender and mash. Mix with the rest of the ingredients to make a dough, adding a little water if necessary. Form into small balls and deep fry. Serve with a gravy or dal.

Cauliflower Balls (*Phūlgobi kofta*)

½ kilo (1 lb.) cauliflower
salt
small piece ginger, finely
  chopped
1 green chilli, sliced
4 cloves garlic, finely chopped
½ teaspoon garam masala
gram flour

Wash the cauliflower, break into sprigs and cook till tender in the minimum of salted water. Mash well. Add the ginger, chilli, garlic, garam masala and enough gram flour to make a stiff mixture. Roll up into balls and deep fry. Serve hot with a curry or curd.

Carrot Salad (*Kachūmbar*)

250 g. (½ lb.) carrots
1 tablespoon ghee
½ teaspoon mustard seed
salt
chilli powder
lemon juice

Wash the carrots and cut in small pieces. Heat the ghee and fry the mustard seeds till they jump. Add the carrots and a little water and cook gently till nearly tender. Sprinkle with salt, chilli powder and lemon juice and serve hot or cold.

Beetroot Salad

1 beetroot
a few spring onions, chopped
1 tomato, chopped
1 green chilli, sliced
salt
lemon juice

133

Boil the beetroot till tender and cut in cubes. Mix with the spring onions, tomato and chilli and sprinkle with salt and lemon juice.

Capsicum (*Simla mirch*)

1 green capsicum	1 cup fried gram, crushed
ghee	salt
½ teaspoon mustard seed	lemon juice
1 green chilli, sliced	chopped fresh coriander leaf
½ teaspoon turmeric powder	

Wash the capsicum and remove the seeds. Slice. Heat some ghee and fry the mustard seeds till they jump. Add the green chilli, turmeric and fried crushed gram and fry gently for a few minutes. Add the sliced capsicum and fry gently until soft. Sprinkle with salt, lemon juice and coriander leaf.

Vangi

½ kilo (1 lb.) aubergines	a few curry leaves, broken
½ cup grated or desiccated coconut	salt
	tamarind water
2 green chillies, sliced	3 tablespoons ghee
1 teaspoon brown sugar	chopped fresh coriander leaf
½ teaspoon turmeric powder	

Wash the brinjals (aubergines) and make lengthwise slits along them. Mix the coconut with the rest of the ingredients, adding a little tamarind water to make a paste. Stuff the brinjals with the masala. Heat the ghee and fry them gently with the cover on the pan, turning to prevent burning. Cook till tender and serve garnished with a sprinkling of coriander leaf. This recipe is from Maharashtra.

Corn Kabab

corn-cobs (*buta*)	1 onion, finely chopped
½ cup curd	½ teaspoon chilli powder
1 teaspoon garam masala	salt

Wash the corn-cobs and put on skewers. Beat the curd and stir in the rest of the ingredients. Smear over the corn cobs and barbecue or cook under the grill till tender. Eat with chutney. The kababs may also be basted with ghee.

Kashmiri Cutlets

½ kilo (1 lb.) potatoes
salt
2 tablespoons semolina (suji)
½ cup peas
½ cup carrots, sliced
½ cup green beans, sliced
2 tablespoons ghee
1 onion, sliced
3 cm. (1 inch) piece ginger, finely chopped
1 green chilli, sliced

a few mint leaves, chopped
1 teaspoon garam masala
1 teaspoon cumin powder
½ cup mixed nuts, chopped
1 tablespoon sultanas
½ teaspoon saffron in 1 tablespoon milk
yogurt
1 egg, beaten
breadcrumbs

Boil the potatoes in salted water till soft. Peel and mash. Knead with the semolina to a smooth mixture. Meanwhile cook the other vegetables in a little water till tender. Heat the ghee and fry the onion till golden. Add the spices except the saffron and salt to taste and the cooked vegetables and fry gently till the moisture is driven off. Mix the nuts and sultanas together and lightly fry. Then blend with the saffron and a little yogurt. Roll out the potato mixture carefully, keeping a little aside. Make the mixture into a rectangle and put on the vegetables, leaving a margin of 2–3 cm. (1 inch) all round the edge. Put the nut mixture in the centre of the vegetable. Now carefully roll up the potato and seal the edges, using the potato that was kept aside to fill in any gaps. Brush all over with the egg and spread with breadcrumbs. Bake in the oven till golden as it is or wrapped in foil. Serve hot with a curry or chutney.

Much of the food of Kerala has coconut as its base. The bland, balanced dishes that follow are an excellent addition to a vegetarian or meat meal.

Eriseri

250 g. (½ lb.) yam or banana
salt
½ teaspoon turmeric powder
½ teaspoon pepper

1 cup grated or desiccated
coconut
1 tablespoon ghee or coconut oil
1 teaspoon mustard seed
a few curry leaves

Peel and wash the yam or banana and cut in small cubes. Cook in a little salted water with the turmeric. Grind the pepper and half a cup of coconut together to make a paste, adding a little water. Stir into the boiling yam or banana and cook till tender. Heat the ghee and fry the mustard seeds till they jump. Add the rest of the coconut and the curry leaves and fry till the coconut is golden. Add to the eriseri. Stir in a little more melted ghee and mix the dish well.

Perakku

This Kerala dish is made on Vishu, the first day of the Kerala New Year.

½ cup grated or desiccated
coconut
½ teaspoon chilli powder
½ teaspoon mustard seed
salt

½ cup cucumber, finely
chopped
½ cup mango, well chopped, or
lemon slices

Mix all the ingredients together with enough salt to taste. Serve with eriseri.

Puzukku

½ cup whole green gram
6 bananas, sliced and peeled
salt
1 tablespoon brown sugar or
jaggery

½ teaspoon turmeric powder
½ cup grated or desiccated
coconut
½ teaspoon chilli powder
1 teaspoon coconut oil or ghee

Roast the gram for a few minutes. Put 4–5 cups of water in a pan and boil the gram till almost tender. Add the bananas, salt to taste, sugar, turmeric powder, coconut and chilli powder. Cook till much of the liquid is driven off and the gram and bananas are tender. Stir in the oil or ghee and serve with curd, rice or breads.

Curd (Yogurt)

Raitas are India's gift to lovers of salad and are also a pleasing and complementary accompaniment to a hotter or spicier dish. (See *Dahi* under *Basic Ingredients*.)

Spiced Curd (*Raita*)

1 tablespoon ghee
2 cloves garlic, finely chopped
½ teaspoon turmeric powder
½ teaspoon salt
2 cups yogurt

½ teaspoon paprika or chilli powder
1 tablespoon chopped coriander leaf

Heat the ghee and fry the garlic, turmeric and salt for two minutes. Beat the yogurt till smooth and stir in the paprika and coriander leaf. Cook gently for another five minutes. Chill and serve as a chutney with rice and curry. Any finely cut vegetables can be added to this basic recipe. Garam masala may be substituted for the turmeric.

Mixed Vegetable Raita

2 cups yogurt
salt
½ cup cucumber, finely
  chopped
1 tomato, finely chopped

1 onion, finely chopped
1 green chilli, sliced
pinch cumin powder
pinch black pepper

Beat the yogurt with salt to taste and mix in the vegetables. Sprinkle with the green chilli, cumin and black pepper. Serve chilled.

Aubergine Raita (*Baingan raita*)

1 large aubergine
salt
3 cm. (1 inch) piece ginger
1 green chilli
ghee

4 cloves garlic, finely chopped
2 cups yogurt
pinch turmeric powder
pinch cumin powder

Cut the aubergine into slim rings and sprinkle with salt. Grind the ginger and chilli to make a paste. Smear over the aubergine and fry in ghee till crisp. Beat the garlic into the curd with turmeric and cumin powder. Heat a little more ghee and gently fry the curd mixture. Put in a dish and lay the aubergine slices on top. Serve chilled.

Potato Raita (*Ālū raita*)

250 g. (½ lb.) potatoes, boiled,
  peeled and diced
salt
2 cups yogurt
¼ teaspoon cumin powder
small piece ginger, finely
  chopped

pinch chilli powder
2 tablespoons brown sugar or
  jaggery
½ cup tamarind water

Make alu raita by beating the potato and salt to taste into the curd. Mix the rest of the ingredients with the tamarind water and heat gently till the liquid thickens. Cool the ingredients and serve the tamarind sauce with the raita.

Carrot Raita (*Gājar raita*)

2 carrots, grated
2 tablespoons nuts, crushed
1 green chilli, sliced
2 tablespoons chopped
   coriander leaf

salt
2 cups yogurt

Mix all the ingredients together with salt to taste.

Banana Raita (*Kela raita*)

1 tablespoon sultanas
ghee
1 teaspoon mustard seeds
2 bananas, sliced

pinch garam masala
½ teaspoon chilli powder
salt
2 cups yogurt

Fry the sultanas in ghee with the mustard seeds till they jump. Drain off the ghee and mix into the curd with the other ingredients. This recipe comes from Maharashtra where the word *raita* is derived from *rai* (mustard seed).

Tomato and Onion Raita
(*Tamātar pīāz raita*)

1 tablespoon ghee
1 teaspoon mustard seed
a few curry leaves
small piece ginger, finely
   chopped

1 green chilli, sliced
4 spring onions, sliced
2 tomatoes, chopped
2 cups yogurt
chopped fresh coriander leaf

Heat the ghee and fry the mustard seeds till they jump. Add the rest of the ingredients and fry gently till the onions begin to turn golden. Beat into the curd and serve sprinkled with coriander leaf.

These dahi badas or vadas come from Uttar Pradesh state.

Mutton Dahi Bada

250 g. (½ lb.) minced mutton
salt
1 green chilli, sliced
small piece ginger, finely
  chopped
a few mint leaves, chopped
1 teaspoon coriander powder
1 teaspoon cumin powder

ghee
2 cups tamarind water
2 tablespoons brown sugar or
  jaggery
1 teaspoon garam masala
pinch chilli powder
1–2 cups yogurt
chopped coriander leaf

Boil the mince in a little salted water till tender and dry. Mix well with the chilli, ginger, mint, coriander powder and cumin powder. Knead the mixture till smooth. Form into flat round cakes and deep fry till golden. Drain and keep aside. Make the tamarind water with hot water and dissolve the brown sugar in it with salt, garam masala and chilli powder. Put the badas in a dish and pour over the spiced tamarind water. Cover with the curd and sprinkle with coriander leaf.

Ginger Curd (*Dahi adrak*)

3 cm. (1 inch) piece ginger
2 tablespoons grated or
  desiccated coconut
1 green chilli, sliced
1 onion, chopped
1 tablespoon chopped coriander
  leaf

1 cup yogurt
salt
brown sugar
lemon juice

Grind the ginger, coconut, chilli, onion and coriander to a paste and beat into the curd with salt, sugar and lemon juice to taste. Serve as a chutney or raita.

Curd Curry

In the North, curd curry is thick. In Gujerat where this recipe comes from the curry is more liquid and served with a dry dal or beans. The dish goes very well with a dry meat or chicken curry.

4 cups yogurt .
1 tablespoon gram flour (besan)
3 cm. (1 inch) piece ginger,
    finely chopped
2 green chillies, sliced
1 tablespoon ghee
1 teaspoon mustard seed
4 cloves
3 cm. (1 inch) piece cinnamon,
    broken
a few curry leaves
250 g. (½ lb.) Lady Fingers,
    chopped
salt
1 teaspoon brown sugar
chopped fresh coriander leaf

Mix the curd with the gram flour and stir in 4–6 cups of water. Heat the ghee and fry the mustard seeds till they jump. Add the rest of the spices and fry for two more minutes. Pour in the curd and gram flour mixture and vegetable and bring to the boil. Lower the heat and simmer gently, stirring occasionally. Add salt to taste and the sugar. Cook for 15–20 minutes and serve garnished with coriander leaf.

Malai Kofta Curry

250 g. (½ lb.) potatoes, boiled,
    peeled and mashed
½ cup curd cheese
1 tablespoon sultanas, fried
1 tablespoon cornflour·
salt
ghee or oil for frying
1 onion, sliced
3 cm. (1 inch) piece ginger,
    finely chopped
2 cloves garlic, finely chopped
1 tablespoon tomato purée
½ teaspoon chilli powder
½ cup yogurt
2 tablespoons cream

Mix the potato, cheese, sultanas and cornflour and salt to taste. Roll up into small balls with a little more flour. Deep fry till golden. Make a sauce by frying the onion till golden in a little more ghee. Add the ginger, garlic, tomato purée and chilli powder with salt to taste. Fry for two minutes then add the beaten curd with a little water and simmer gently. When the sauce is thick put in the koftas and heat through. Add the cream just before serving.

Dahi Badas

1 cup urhad dal
3 cm. (1 inch) piece ginger, finely chopped
1 teaspoon salt
½ teaspoon chilli powder

ghee or oil for frying
½ teaspoon cumin powder
1 green chilli, sliced
2 cups yogurt

Soak the dal overnight and drain next day. Grind to a fine paste and mix in the ginger, salt and chilli powder. Make up into small balls and then flatten to form badas. Deep fry till golden and put in cold water for ten minutes. Meanwhile beat the cumin and green chilli into the curd. Squeeze the badas dry and put in the curd.

Savouries

These dishes may be included in a teatime menu or may be part of a lunch, dinner or even breakfast. They are useful in providing appetizing food where a full meal is not required.

Stuffed Meat Pasties (*Samosa*)

1½ cups wholewheat or plain flour
ghee for frying
1 onion, finely chopped
small piece ginger, finely chopped
1 cup minced meat
1 tablespoon peas
1 teaspoon salt
1 teaspoon coriander powder
1 teaspoon cumin powder
½ teaspoon paprika or chilli powder
1 tablespoon chopped coriander leaf
½ teaspoon garam masala
1 potato, boiled, peeled and and mashed
2 teaspoons lemon juice

Sieve the flour with a pinch of salt. Rub in 2 tablespoons of melted ghee. Add enough water (5 tablespoons) to make a smooth dough.

Knead for a few minutes, cover with a damp cloth and allow to stand. Heat 2 tablespoons of ghee and fry the onion. Stir in the ginger, mince, peas, salt and spices and fry for two minutes. Add the potato and lemon juice and fry for a few more minutes. Cool. Knead the dough again and make into small balls, rolling out each one quite thin. Cut in half and lay the pieces over each other. Press lightly together, roll as thin as possible to make a semicircle. Put a portion of the filling on one half of the pastry, moisten the edges and fold the other half over. Press the edges well together and deep fry in hot ghee till crisp and lightly golden. Serve with a chutney. The pastry may be made more flaky by rolling out and adding two more tablespoons of ghee, roll up again and knead. A variety of stuffings may be used to taste.

Savoury Fritters (*Bhajia*)

2 cups gram flour (besan)
1 onion, finely chopped
1 tablespoon yogurt
1 teaspoon coriander powder
1 green chilli, sliced
1 tablespoon chopped coriander leaf
$\frac{1}{2}$ teaspoon baking powder
salt
ghee or oil for frying

Mix the flour with the onion and curd and enough water to make a creamy batter. Add the rest of the ingredients and beat well. Allow to stand. Heat ghee to smoking heat and deep-fry spoonfuls of the batter till golden. Serve with chutney.

Bengal Cutlets

1 cup gram flour
$\frac{1}{2}$ teaspoon baking powder
salt
1 potato
1 carrot
3 tablespoons peas
a few pieces of cauliflower
ghee
$\frac{1}{2}$ teaspoon mustard seed
$\frac{1}{2}$ teaspoon fenugreek seed
$\frac{1}{2}$ teaspoon cumin seed
$\frac{1}{2}$ teaspoon coriander powder
$\frac{1}{2}$ teaspoon garam masala
1 tablespoon chopped nuts
1 tablespoon sultanas

Mix the gram flour, baking powder and a pinch of salt with enough water to make a creamy batter. Boil the vegetables in a little water till tender, then mash together. Heat a tablespoon of ghee and fry the seeds for two minutes. Add the rest of the spices and the nuts and sultanas and fry till the sultanas puff up. Mix well with the mashed vegetable. Form into cutlets, dip in the batter and deep fry till golden. Serve with chutney and curd.

Potato Patties

4–6 potatoes
3 cm. (1 inch) piece ginger
2 green chillies
1 tablespoon coriander leaves
1 tablespoon crushed nuts
2 tablespoons grated or
  desiccated coconut

2 tablespoons gram flour
  (besan)
salt
lemon juice
ghee or oil for deep frying

Boil, peel and mash the potato. Grind the ginger and green chilli and mix all the other ingredients and the potato. Make up the mixture into patties and deep fry till golden. Serve with chutney.

Sada Dosa

This is the plain but popular pancake from South India.

2 cups rice flour
1 cup urhad dal flour
salt

1 tablespoon yogurt
1 teaspoon cumin or caraway
  seed

Mix the flours, salt and seed to taste with the yogurt and enough water to make a fairly thin batter. Allow to stand for 6–8 hours. Heat an iron hot plate (tava) and grease it a little. Pour two tablespoons of batter on to the tava starting from the centre of the plate. Cook on a slow fire until the upper side dries. Turn and cook again. Really thin dosas only need cooking on one side. Serve hot with chutney.

Shakahari Pancake

This pancake is like the dosa but comes from the West in Maharashtra.

1 cup rice flour
2 tablespoons gram flour
  (besan)
1 onion, finely chopped
1 tablespoon chopped coriander
  leaf

1 green chilli, sliced
small piece ginger, finely
  chopped
salt

Mix all the ingredients with enough water to make a pancake batter. Heat the iron plate and cook on both sides till golden. Serve with chutney.

Vegetable Pasties (*Shingara*)

There is a pasty made in Bengal called the shingara. It is made like samosa but use plain flour (maida). Make up the filling as follows:

2 potatoes, boiled, peeled and
  mashed
a few sprigs cauliflower, boiled
2 tablespoons peas, cooked
ghee
3 cm. (1 inch) piece ginger,
  finely chopped
3 cm. (1 inch) piece cinnamon,
  broken
2 cloves

1 teaspoon cumin seeds
1 green chilli, sliced
1 green cardamom, crushed
1 teaspoon poppy seeds
1 tablespoon chopped nuts
1 tablespoon sultanas
1 tablespoon chopped coriander
  leaf
salt

Mash the vegetables. Heat the ghee and fry the masala ingredients for a few minutes. Heat another tablespoon of ghee and fry the nuts, sultanas and coriander with salt to taste till the sultanas puff up. Mix all the ingredients together. Make up a shingara dough with plain flour as under Stuffed Meat Pasties. Stuff with the vegetable filling.

Fried Cashew Nuts

3 tablespoons gram flour
  (besan)
½ teaspoon turmeric powder
1 teaspoon cumin powder
pinch baking powder

pinch chilli powder
salt
250 g. (½ lb.) whole cashew nuts
ghee or oil for frying

Mix the batter ingredients together with a little water to form a thick batter. Stir in a teaspoon of hot ghee and leave to stand for fifteen minutes. Dip each nut in the batter and deep fry till golden. Drain and store in a airtight container. These make a delicious nibble with drinks or as a little snack.

Mysore Abode

1½ cups gram flour
1 onion, finely chopped
1 green chilli, sliced
2 tablespoons grated or
  desiccated coconut

1 tablespoon coriander leaf
salt
ghee or oil for frying

Mix all the ingredients together with a little water if necessary to form thin cutlets. Deep fry till golden. Serve with chutney.

Banana Bhajias

1 cup rice flour
¼ cup urhad dal flour
¼ cup gram flour (besan)
½ teaspoon chilli powder

salt
6 bananas
ghee or oil for frying

Mix the batter ingredients together with enough water to make a thick batter. Leave for half an hour. Slice the bananas and dip in the batter. Deep fry till golden. Serve with chutney. This recipe is from Kerala.

Savoury Paras

1 cup plain flour
1 tablespoon gram flour
¼ teaspoon chilli powder
¼ teaspoon turmeric powder
½ teaspoon cumin powder

1 dessertspoon ghee
2 tablespoons ground peanuts
salt
oil for deep frying

Mix the flour and spices with the ghee and ground peanuts. Add enough water to make a stiff dough, sprinkling salt to taste. Cover with a damp cloth and allow to stand for half an hour. Roll out the dough on a floured board about $\frac{1}{2}$ cm. thick. Cut into diamond shapes and deep fry till golden. Serve with curd, beaten with a little spice and salad vegetables.

Sweetmeats and Sweet Dishes

In the noble establishments of seventh-century India, a great variety of desserts were offered. These included scented curds, creamy cheeses (*kilata*), balls of rice or wheat coated with sugar, thin slices of coconut and various spices which were steam-boiled (dammed) or fried in butter. Seeds fried in oil were served. Sugar-cane, refined or moulded into oval loaves, provided the base for sweet dishes (*modaka*) containing molasses, curds, ghee and pepper. These were followed by fruits, especially the mango, curds, whey and salted rice. Just as today, milk foods were very popular, flavoured with spices and camphor. Honey was reserved for special occasions.

Pistachio Nut Milk Sweet (*Pistā barfi*)

227 g. (½ lb. approx) sugar
1 cup water
280 g. (10 oz.) dried milk
8 white cardamoms, skinned
    and crushed

300 g. (12 oz.) pistachio nuts,
    crushed
green colouring

Make a syrup by boiling the sugar and water briskly. The syrup is ready when a tiny drop forms a ball when put on the edge of a cold dish. Stir the rest of the ingredients together, adding the colouring slowly so as to make the mixture light green. Turn on to a greased dish. Cut when cool.

Ginger Barfi (*Adrak barfi*)

3–4 tablespoons ghee
4 tablespoons semolina (suji)
250 g. (½ lb.) fresh ginger,
    crushed

250 g. (½ lb.) sugar
6 white cardamoms, skinned
    and crushed

Heat the ghee and fry the semolina and ginger till golden. Add the sugar and cardamom and cook gently till the mixture becomes sticky. Turn on to a greased plate and cut when cool.

Banana Halva (*Kela halva*)

8 ripe banas
sugar

ghee

Boil the bananas till soft and mash. Make a syrup as for Barfi and cook the banana in the syrup till the whole forms one mass. Stir continuously. Add spoonfuls of ghee, stirring all the time, till the mass comes away clean from the sides of the pan. Turn on to a greased dish and cut when set.

Beetroot Halva (*Chukunda halva*)

250 g. (½ lb.) beetroot
ghee

1 teaspoon powdered cardamom
    seed

4 tablespoons sugar   chopped nuts
4 tablespoons dried milk
   powder

Grate the peeled beet and fry in a little ghee for a few minutes. Add
a little water and continue cooking. Add the sugar and milk powder.
When the mixture is nearly dry add the cardamom. Cook gently till
the halva forms balls easily in the hands. Roll up with greased fingers
and garnish with chopped nuts.

Banana Fritter

2 ripe bananas   1 teaspoon powdered cardamom
½ teaspoon baking powder   seed
3 tablespoons flour   milk
2 tablespoons brown sugar or   ghee or oil for frying
   jaggery

Mash the bananas and mix with the baking powder, flour, sugar and
cardamom. Add enough milk to form a thick batter. Deep-fry spoonfuls of the batter till golden.

Gram and Khoya Sweet (*Pantua*)

This sweet from Bengal uses Bengal gram and milk.

250 g. (½ lb.) Bengal gram   ghee for frying
250 g. (½ lb.) khoya (see *Basic*   2 cups sugar
   Ingredients)   rosewater
2 tablespoons semolina (suji)
2 teaspoons ground cardamom
   seed

Boil the gram till tender. Drain and grind to a paste. Add the khoya,
semolina and cardamom. Knead well and form into small balls.
Flatten a little and deep fry till golden. Make a thin syrup with the
sugar and a cup of water. Put the pantua in the syrup and sprinkle the
dish with rosewater.

Raj Bhog

2 cups panir or cottage cheese
1 teaspoon saffron, dissolved in
  a little milk
1 tablespoon semolina (suji)

1 teaspoon baking powder
1 cup sliced nuts
sugar
rosewater

Beat the panir with the saffron liquid. Mix in the semolina and baking powder and knead to make a smooth mixture. Form balls of the mixture around some nuts. Make up a syrup as for barfi and boil. Put in the balls while the syrup is still thin and wait for them to swell up. Let the syrup thicken a little, sprinkle with rosewater and serve cool. Raj bhog sweet is made in Uttar Pradesh.

Sweet Potato Balls

2 sweet potatoes
2 tablespoons wheat flour (ata)
salt

$\frac{1}{2}$ cup grated or desiccated
  coconut
$\frac{1}{2}$ cup brown sugar

Boil the sweet potatoes and mash. Knead well with the flour and salt. Make into small balls. Mix the coconut and sugar, make a depression in each potato ball and fill with this stuffing. Close up carefully. Put the balls in boiling water and cook till they rise up in the water. Remove and drain. Roll in some more coconut and serve with cream and syrup.

Ras Vadas

250 g. ($\frac{1}{2}$ lb.) urhad dal flour
$\frac{1}{2}$ kilo (1 lb.) khoya (see *Basic
  Ingredients*)
2 tablespoons sultanas
1 tablespoon almonds, blanched
  and chopped

ghee
sugar
rosewater

Mix the flour with the khoya. Fry the sultanas and nuts in ghee till the sultanas puff up. Make the dough up into small balls and fill with the nuts and almonds. Roll up and deep fry in ghee till golden. Make a syrup as for barfi and soak the balls in the syrup. Sprinkle on rosewater.

Cottage Cheese Sweet (*Sandesh*)

2 cups panir or cottage cheese
yogurt

chopped pistachio nuts
¼ teaspoon ground cardamom

Knead the cheese with a little yogurt to make a soft dough. Spread the dough on a slightly buttered hot plate or heavy pan and steam. When the dough hardens, sprinkle with the nuts and cardamom. Cut in diamond shapes to serve.

Fried Vermicelli (*Saska Kaboli*)

350 g. (12 oz.) vermicelli
ghee
1 cup milk or water
4–6 tablespoons sugar
¼ cup rosewater
½ cup pistachio nuts, sliced

½ cup almonds, blanched and
  sliced
½ cup raisins
½ cup sultanas
6 cardamoms, ground seeds

Brown the vermicelli in ghee. Add the milk and sugar and simmer very gently till the vermicelli is cooked. Remove from the fire and stir in rosewater. Meanwhile heat some more ghee and fry the nuts, fruits and cardamom for a few minutes. Serve sprinkled with the fried nuts and fruit.

Sweet Stuffed Puris (*Gujiya*)

250 g. (½ lb.) plain flour (maida)
ghee
4 tablespoons khoya
2 tablespoons sultanas
2 tablespoons almonds,
  blanched and chopped

1 tablespoon grated or
  desiccated coconut
3 tablespoons sugar
ghee or oil for frying

Sift the flour with a little ghee and enough water to make a soft dough as for puris. Mix the filling ingredients together. Make the dough into balls, roll out thinly and put a little of the filling on one half. Fold over and seal the edges with milk. Make a syrup as for barfi. Fry the gujiyas in ghee or oil till golden and dip in the thick syrup. Serve cool.

Semolina Sweet (*Sūji beveca*)

250 g. (½ lb.) semolina (suji)
1 cup coconut milk or
   creamed coconut
4 eggs, beaten
3 tablespoons almonds,
   blanched

2 tablespoons ghee
¼ teaspoon caraway seed
salt
brown sugar

Mix the suji with the coconut milk and leave to soak for an hour. Meanwhile beat the eggs and grind the almonds to a paste. Add the eggs, almond paste, ghee, caraway seed, pinch of salt and sugar to the suji. Put in a buttered baking dish and bake in a moderate oven.

Lemon Pudding

1 tablespoon cornflour
2 cups water
juice of 1 lemon

sugar
2 eggs

Mix the cornflour carefully with the water, stirring and adding it gradually so that no lumps are formed. Add the lemon juice and sugar to taste. Beat the eggs well and mix with the cornflour. Put in a piece of lemon peel and simmer gently until the mixture is thick. Remove the peel, pour into a mould and chill.

Custard Pudding

2 cups milk
small piece cinnamon
6 eggs
sugar

12 almonds, blanched and
   sliced
nutmeg

Boil the milk for a few minutes with the cinnamon or a piece of lemon peel. Cool and remove the cinnamon or peel. Separate the six egg yolks and beat well in a bowl. Pour in the cooled boiled milk. Add sugar to taste and the nuts. Finally beat the egg whites to a stiff froth and add to the custard. Stir well, pour into a buttered oven dish, sprinkle with nutmeg and bake till firm.

Frosted Plantains

½–1 kilo (1–2 lb.) plantains or
  large bananas
ghee

salt
1 cup water
½ cup sugar

Slice the bananas on the slant. Fry in a little ghee but do not brown
too much. Meanwhile dissolve the salt in the water. Put in a teaspoon
at a time of salt water into the pan where the bananas are frying.
Dissolve the sugar in a cup of water and boil to make a thick syrup.
Dip the cooked plantain in the syrup and allow to cool and frost with
sugar.

Chutneys and Pickles

Chutneys

Green Chilli

Cut and seed green chillies, mix with finely chopped ginger, salt, lemon juice and chilli powder.

Garlic

Mix grated or desiccated coconut and chillies with finely chopped garlic.

Coconut

½ cup grated or desiccated
  coconut
juice of 1 lemon
1 teaspoon brown sugar
2 green chillies, sliced
3 cm. (1 inch) piece ginger

4 cloves garlic
2 tablespoons chopped coriander
  leaf
½ teaspoon turmeric powder
1 teaspoon cumin seeds
salt

Grind all the ingredients to make a paste with a little water.
This chutney from Maharashtra can be made the typical South
Indian way by adding the following to the same amount of coconut:

½ teaspoon cumin seed
small piece ginger
2 tablespoons coriander leaf
small piece stoned tamarind
salt
2 tablespoons lemon juice

½ teaspoon chilli powder
ghee
½ teaspoon mustard seed
2 green chillies, sliced
a few curry leaves

Grind the coconut with the cumin, ginger, coriander leaf and tamarind. Add salt to taste, lemon juice and chilli powder. Heat the ghee
and fry the mustard seeds till they jump. Add the chilli and curry
leaves. Stir all together, adding a few drops of water if necessary.

Onion

1 onion, chopped
2 tablespoons grated or
  desiccated coconut
1 tablespoon peanuts

small piece ginger
small piece tamarind
salt
chilli powder

Grind all the ingredients with a little water to make a chutney paste.

Channa Dal

2 tablespoons channa dal
2 tablespoons coriander leaf
2 green chillies
½ cup coconut, grated or
  desiccated

small piece ginger
salt
lemon juice

Soak the dal overnight. Next day, drain and grind to a paste with the rest of the ingredients. This is how it is made in Bihar. For a more southern flavour grind the dal with a tablespoon of tamarind. Heat a tablespoon of ghee and fry ½ teaspoon mustard seed, a few curry leaves, a red chilli and mix with the dal paste with salt to taste. Add a little coconut if preferred.

Coriander

1 cup coriander leaves	2 green chillies
1 cup chopped spring onions	3 cm. (1 inch) piece ginger
1 teaspoon salt	lemon juice

Grind the ingredients together, adding a little brown sugar if a sweet taste is required.

Sultana

10 cloves garlic	2 teaspoons salt
3 cm. (1 inch) piece ginger	1 teaspoon cumin seed
2 cups sultanas	2 teaspoons chilli powder
½ cup dates, stoned and chopped	2 teaspoons garam masala
250 g. (½ lb.) sugar	1 cup vinegar

Grind the garlic and ginger. Mix all the ingredients with the vinegar and cook gently till a thick chutney is formed, allowing for thickening while cooling. Bottle when cold.

Ginger

250 g. (½ lb.) brown sugar or jaggery	300–500 g. (12–16 oz.) ginger
900 ml. (1½ pints) vinegar	3 cloves garlic
2 red chillies	1 cup sultanas
1 teaspoon fenugreek seed	1 tablespoon salt

Boil the sugar in two thirds of the vinegar to form a syrup. Roast the chilli and fenugreek seed for a few minutes. Grind with the ginger, garlic, sultanas. Mix in with the syrup, the rest of the vinegar and salt.

Cook together and bottle when cool. The chutney may be used after two weeks.

Tomato Kasaundi

½ kilo (1 lb.) ripe tomatoes
ghee or mustard oil for frying
1 teaspoon mustard seed
1 teaspoon cumin seed
½ teaspoon turmeric powder
½ teaspoon chilli powder

2 green chillies, sliced
2 cloves garlic, finely chopped
2 tablespoons brown sugar
2 teaspoons salt
½ cup vinegar
½ cup oil

Steam the tomatoes till they become a pulp. Heat the ghee and fry the mustard, cumin, turmeric and chilli powder till the mustard seeds begin to jump. Add the tomato pulp and the rest of the ingredients and cook gently till the oil comes to the top. Serve cold. Kasaundi will keep for a few days with the oil on the surface.

Pickles

Summertime is a good time to make a pickle as the sunlight helps the pickle to mature.

Lime in Oil

12 lemons
salt
2 tablespoons mustard oil
1 teaspoon turmeric powder

2 teaspoons garam masala
2 teaspoons chilli powder
1 tablespoon fennel or aniseed
2 teaspoons mustard seed

Cut the lemons in pieces and allow to dry. Sprinkle with plenty of salt. Heat the oil and fry the masala ingredients till the mustard seeds begin to jump. Cover the lemon pieces with the masala and simmer all together for a few minutes. Fill bottles with the pickle, leaving room to top up with a tablespoon or more of mustard oil. The rest of the oil is put in after a week of leaving the pickle in the sun. Stir daily.

Lime (Sweet)

12 lemons
salt
1 cup vinegar

2 cups brown sugar or jaggery
chilli powder

Cut the lemon in slices and allow to dry. Sprinkle well with salt and keep overnight. Next day boil the lemon in a little water till the skin is tender. Remove and drain. Heat the vinegar, sugar and chilli to make a syrup. Add the lemon slices and cook till the syrup thickens. Cool and bottle. Stir every two or three days. The pickle may be used in two weeks.

Cauliflower

1 kilo (2 lb.) cauliflower, cut in small pieces
1 tablespoon mustard oil
1 tablespoon mustard seed
2 teaspoons turmeric powder

1 teaspoon chilli powder
2 teaspoons garam masala
5 cm. (2 inch) piece ginger, finely chopped
1 tablespoon salt

Boil the cauliflower pieces in a little water for a few moments, remove and drain. Heat the oil and fry the rest of the ingredients till the mustard seeds jump. Mix well with the cauliflower and bottle. Stand in the sun for 5–6 days, stirring occasionally.

Drinks and Soups

The sage Kalidasa (fourth century) tells us that when a guest was expected a chair was made ready and a special drink (*madhuparka*) offered. This was made of sugar, ghee, curds, herbs and honey (*madhu*). This hydromel was reserved for all special occasions. Women were given it to drink when five months pregnant, the eldest son's lips were moistened with it at the time of birth. Students were offered it when they took leave of their gurus and the bridegroom was offered some when he arrived at the home of his future father-in-law on the morning of the wedding.

Lime Yogurt Refresher (*Nimbū lassi*)

Lassi, a drink made with yogurt, is one of the most popular drinks in India. Endless combinations of yogurt, water, herbs and flavourings can be made to make your own lassi. In the summer a really refreshing as well as thirst-quenching drink can be made by beating two dessertspoons of yogurt with a glass of water. Put in ice and a few drops of lime juice or lemon juice.

Mango Payasam

Skin and stone some mangoes and boil the pulp with a little water. Make a syrup with brown sugar and water and add to the mango. Simmer gently and put in tablespoons of coconut milk or creamed coconut to taste. Cook together. Cool and stir in sultanas, sliced nuts and crushed cardamom seeds. Again, try other combinations of fruit to make this nourishing payasam.

Strawberry Drink

Mix two tablespoons of mashed strawberries with a tall glass of milk. Add lemon juice and ice.

Vegetable Drink

For those who like a cold vegetable drink, boil some vegetables in a little water and mash. Add salt, pepper or chilli powder, vinegar or tamarind water, chopped coriander leaf and mint. Stir with a little water and add ice.

Conjis are thick nourishing drinks which can be drunk hot or cold as a pick-me-up.

Methi Seed Conji

2 teaspoons fenugreek seeds
½ cup rice, washed
salt

½ cup thick coconut milk or creamed coconut
brown sugar

Steep the fenugreek seeds (methi) in half a cup of water for six hours. Boil in a cup of water till soft. Add the rice, 2 cups of water and salt to taste. Simmer till the grains soften then add the coconut milk. Stir in sufficient sugar or jaggery to make it sweet or add ground spices if a savoury drink is preferred.

Cereal Conji

1 cup wheat or other cereal
1½ cups coconut milk or coconut cream

2 cardamoms, ground seeds
brown sugar

Boil the wheat in 3–4 cups water till the grains are soft. Pour in the coconut milk. Sprinkle the cardamom and add enough sugar to taste.

Hot Spicy Soup (*Rasam*)

½ cup tur dal
2 green chillies, sliced
4 tomatoes, chopped
½ tablespoon ghee

1 teaspoon mustard seed
a few curry leaves
½ teaspoon turmeric powder
salt

Boil the dal till soft. Add six cups of water and put in the green chillies and tomatoes. Heat the ghee and fry the mustard seed and spices till they jump. Add to the rasam with salt to taste. Simmer gently for fifteen minutes and serve as a drink or soup.

Dal Mulligatawny

1 cup masur dal or lentils
½ teaspoon cumin seed
2 red chillies
6 cloves garlic
½ teaspoon saffron, soaked in a
   little warm water

salt
ghee
1 onion, sliced

Wash the dal and soak for half an hour. Grind the cumin, chillies and garlic. Boil the dal till tender. Add the ground ingredients, saffron and salt to taste. Heat the ghee and fry the onion till golden. Drain and add to the soup. Simmer for two minutes.

Chicken Mulligatawny

1 chicken
6 peppercorns
1 teaspoon turmeric powder
small piece ginger
2 teaspoons coriander seed

1 red chilli
ghee
1 onion, sliced
salt
sliced lemon

Cut the chicken in pieces and boil gently in water. Grind the masala ingredients to make a paste. Mix the paste with the broth and simmer till the meat is tender. Strain off the liquid. Heat a little ghee and fry the onion till golden. Add salt to taste and stir both into the soup. Allow the soup to boil and serve with slices of lemon.

Mutton Mulligatawny

½ kilo (1 lb.) sliced mutton
2 tablespoons peanuts
2 tablespoons almonds,
  blanched
1 teaspoon cumin seed
1 teaspoon mustard seed
1 teaspoon turmeric powder

2–3 tablespoons channa dal
ghee
1 onion, sliced
salt
½ cup coconut milk or creamed
  coconut

Boil the meat in enough water to make a soup. Grind the masala ingredients and stir into the broth. Heat some ghee and fry the onion till golden. Add to the soup with salt to taste and the coconut milk. Boil all together and serve with slices of lemon.

Chicken Pepperwater

1 chicken
2 red chillies
½ teaspoon cumin seed
10 peppercorns
2 teaspoons coriander seed

½ teaspoon mustard seed
ghee
1 onion, sliced
salt

Cut the chicken in pieces and put in a stewpan. Grind the masala ingredients with a little water to make a paste and add to the chicken. Add enough water to cover and boil the chicken till tender. Heat some ghee and fry the onion till golden. Pour into the chicken and season with salt. Cook for a few more minutes and serve the broth.

Chicken and Pumpkin Soup

1 chicken
2 onions, sliced
3–4 tomatoes, chopped
a few cardamoms
½ teaspoon turmeric powder
salt

chilli powder
3 cm. (1 inch) piece ginger,
  finely chopped
3–4 cups cubed pumpkin or
  marrow

Cut the chicken and put in a pan. Cover with the rest of the ingredients and enough water to make a soup. Simmer gently till the meat is tender. Cut the meat from the bones, chop finely and return to the soup. Serve hot.

Jal Jira

4 tablespoons tamarind pulp   pinch chilli powder
4 tablespoons mint, chopped   salt
$\frac{1}{2}$ teaspoon cumin powder   brown sugar

Soak the tamarind in six glasses of water for half an hour and strain off the juice. Grind the mint with the rest of the ingredients and stir into the tamarind water. Add salt and sugar to taste. This drink can be served as an appetizer either hot or cold. It is very nice served chilled in the summer.

Tales of Deviprasad:
Be Vigilant

Deviprasad warned his boys: 'Never relax your concentration for an instant. Be vigilant at all times. Above all seek to preserve your own integrity.'

'What do you mean by this, master?' questioned one of the boys. Deviprasad replied, 'I mean this: One day the famous cook Ram of Bangalore told his pupils, "My sons, I have taught you all I know save for one thing and that you may only guess by strict and thorough observation of your teacher. Soon it will be time for you to set out on your own account. Put all your effort into this final piece of work." The boys worked hard and when the day came for them to leave Ram he blessed them with tears in his eyes. His last words to them were "Be vigilant at all times."

'Some years later, one of his pupils heard of a great cookery competition being held by a local nobleman. The task was to prepare a dish equal in merit to one of the famous Ram of Bangalore. "Hah! I can win this contest easily," he thought. "Ram himself has taught me all he knew." He went home happy in the knowledge that soon the handsome prize offered by the nobleman would be his.'

'The day came and cooks of all ages took part in the competition, each one producing his own favourite dish. Respected tasters from all over the state whittled them down to six finalists. Then the last six were told: "So far you are the six best, but in spite of this not one of you has even approached the excellence of the famous cook Ram of Bangalore. You are to prepare one more dish each for the final judgement." The young man looked at the other five finalists and saw to his astonishment that one of them was a friend who had also studied under Ram himself. Before he could speak to him, however, the other young man had disappeared silently into the watching crowd.

'The next day, the young man was in a fever of excitement. He had been awake all night. He knew that he had remembered everything that Ram had ever taught him and now he knew that he had prepared his masterpiece. The crowd waited expectantly while the incense was lit and waved in front of the image of the deity. Small portions of all the six final dishes were offered up. Then the tasters retired to a tent nearby. The young man was beside himself with impatience. But the judgement went to the other pupil of the famous Ram. And there stood his old master, Ram himself, the final judge of the contest. "This dish indeed embodies all of my teachings," Ram announced to the crowd.

'The young man was furious, suddenly recalling a forgotten memory. He stepped forward and addressed himself to the assembled gathering. "I protest!" he shouted. "Ram never taught anyone all he knew! He purposely witheld his last secret from all of us. No one can possibly know this!" There was a murmur of disapproval at the young man's rudeness. The nobleman seemed angry. "What does this mean?" he demanded.

'The great Ram came forward. "My lord, this young man is right. I did witheld one secret, the one secret which every pupil of mine had to find for himself. Sire, I wished my pupils to gain full mastery of their art. To do this they had to discover themselves and on making this discovery they had to be themselves at all times. This young man's dish, unlike the one which has won this competition, tastes exactly as I would have made it. I conclude, therefore, that he has not mastered the fullness of my teaching."'

Note on Pronunciation of Indian Words

Indian languages are written phonetically and all the letters are pronounced. Except for 'ch' and 'sh', an 'h' after a consonant should be pronounced separately. 'E' and 'o' are long vowels; 'i' is pronounced long at the end of a word.

Pronounce 'a' as 'u' in the English word 'but'
    'ā' as 'a' in the English word 'father'
    'i' as 'i' in the English word 'bit'
    'ī' as 'ee' in the English word 'meet'
    'u' as 'oo' in the English word 'book'
    'ū' as 'oo' in the English word 'moon'

You will notice a variation in English transliteration of Indian words amongst authors and on the menus in restaurants. This is partly due to the phonetic nature of Indian language alphabets and local changes in pronunciation.

Glossary

ālū	potato
ām	mango
arū	peach
bafat	a way of cooking meat with vegetables
baingan	aubergine, eggplant
barfi	sweet made usually from milk
batāta	potato
bāth	South Indian rice dish
besan	gram flour
Bhagavad Gītā	'The Song of the Lord', part of the *Mahābharata* that contains the teachings of Lord Krishna, an incarnation of the god Vishnu
bhajia	fried savoury in gram flour batter, pakora, pakoda
bhujia	fried greens
bhuna	sauteed meat
channa	yellow peas
chapāti	flat bread made from wholewheat flour and water
chasnidarh	sweet-and-sour style cookery where meat is cooked in a *chasni* (syrup)
chāval	rice
chukunda	beetroot
dahi	yogurt, curd
dāl	split peas
dam	technique of steaming
dosa	spicy pancake (South India)
fūgath	vegetables and meat fried with onions and masala
gājar	carrot
ghee	clarified butter, used since ancient times
gosht	meat
gūda	marrow
halva	heavy sweet made by reducing fruit or vegetable with sugar

jīra	cumin
kabāb	spitted meat, meat or vegetable balls
Kabli channa	Bengal peas
Kashmīri	cooking style of Kashmir, one of the most northern parts of the Indian subcontinent
kela	banana
khichhari	rice and lentils cooked together
khīra	cucumber
khoya	thick milk made by slowly driving off the water
kīma	minced meat
kofta	meat or vegetable ball
korma	food cooked in curd
machchi	fish
Mahābharata	great epic poem of India, said to have been written by the god Ganapati who dictated to the sage Vyasa.
masāla	a mixture of spices used for flavouring and aromatizing food
masūr	red lentils
matar	peas
moli	curry technique using coconut
Mughal (Mogul)	the people who brought to India an Islamic culture from central Asia; the Mughal shahs reigned from 1556–1784
mūng	green peas
murgh	chicken
nān	flat bread baked in Northern India
nargisi	preparations using hard-boiled eggs and vegetables are called *nargisi* (narcissus). See *Nargisi kabāb*.
nimbū	lemon or lime
palak	spinach
parātha	flat bread made from wholewheat flour and fried in ghee
phūlgobi	cauliflower
pīāz	onion
pistā	pistachio nut
pulau	rice first fried in ghee, then cooked in a stock which should be fully absorbed
pūri	small puffed breads fried in ghee
Quran	the holy book of Islam (the Koran)
raita	vegetable in curd (North India)

rajas	in Hindu philosophy, the quality of action
roti	bread
sāg	greens
sambhar	hot lentils, hot masala (South India)
sattva	in Hindu philosophy, the quality of harmony
savia	vermicelli
simla mirch	green pepper, capsicum
sūji	semolina
tamas	in Hindu philosophy, the quality of inertia
tamātar	tomato
tandūri	a form of baking using a clay oven (*tandur*)
tikki	cutlet
urhad	black pea
vindālū	sour curry with vinegar base made in Goa

Where to Buy Indian Ingredients

*Bazaar of India, 1331 University Avenue, Berkeley, California 94702
*Bezjian's Grocery, 4725 Santa Monica Blvd.,
   Los Angeles, California 90029
California Direct Import Co. (Oh's), 2651 Mission St.,
   San Francisco, California 94110
*Haig's Delicacies, 642 Clement St., San Francisco, California 94118
*India Imports & Exports, 10641 West Pico Blvd.,
   Los Angeles, California 90064
*Porter's Food Unlimited, 125 West 11th St., Eugene, Oregon 97401
*Specialty Spice Shop; mail order address: 2757 152nd Avenue, N.E.,
   Redmond, Washington 98052; retail outlet: Pike Place Market,
   Seattle, Washington 98101
*Tarver's Delicacies, De Anza Shopping Center,
   1338 South Mary Avenue, Sunnyvale, California 94087
Wholy Foods, 2999 Shattuck Avenue, Berkeley, California 94705

MIDWEST

*India Gift and Food Store, 1031 Belmont, Chicago, Illinois 60657
*International House of Foods, 440 West Gorham St.,
   Madison, Wisconsin 53703

SOUTH

*Antone's, 2606 South Sheridan, Tulsa, Oklahoma 74129
*Jay Store, 4023 Westheimer, Houston, Texas 77027
Jung's Oriental Foods and Gifts,
   2519 North Fitzburgh, Dallas, Texas 75204
Yoga and Health Center, 2912 Oaklawn, Dallas, Texas 75222

*Aphrodisia, 28 Carmine St., New York, New York 10014

*House of Spices, 76-17 Broadway, Jackson Heights, New York 11373

*India Food and Gourmet, 110 Lexington Ave.,
    New York, New York 10016

*Indian Super Bazaar; mail order address: P.O. Box 1977, Silver Spring,
    Maryland 20902; retail outlets: 3735 Rhode Island, Mt. Rainier,
    20822; International Bazaar, 7720 Wisconsin Avenue, Bethesda, 20014

*Kalpana Indian Groceries, 4275 Main St., Flushing, New York 11355

*K. Kalustyan, Orient Export Trading Corp., 123 Lexington Ave.,
    New York, New York 10016

 T. G. Koryn, Inc., 66 Broad St., Carlstad, New Jersey 07072

*Spice Corner, 904 South 9th, Philadelphia, Pennsylvania 19147

*Spices and Foods Unlimited, Inc., 2018 A Florida Ave., N.W.,
    Washington D.C. 20009

CANADA

*T. Eaton's Co., 190 Yonge St., Toronto 205, Ontario

*S. Enkin Inc., Imports and Exports,
    1201 St. Lawrence, Montreal 18, Quebec

*these will mail order

Bibliography

Mahābharata
Artha Shastra
Quran
Journal of the Royal Asiatic Society 1906
Rigvedic Culture – Abinas Chandra Das, Calcutta, 1925
La Vie Quotidienne dans L'Inde Ancienne – Jeannine Auboyer, Paris, 1961